W9-ACV-097

WHAT PEOPLE ARE SAYING ABOUT *FIX IT!*

Are you just starting a ministry and quickly getting bogged down in all the details and demands? Are you in an active ministry that is growing so quickly that you can't seem to stay caught up? Are you overseeing a long-term ministry that seems to chug along relatively smoothly? If you're in any of these categories, Rob Ketterling has some excellent advice for you. It's never too soon to start implementing his sound structure for your ministry. You're never too busy to benefit from his you/them/God division of responsibility. And it's never too late to review and reevaluate the effectiveness of what you are doing. Whatever your current challenges and problems, Rob's book is certain to help you fix it!

Nancy Alcorn
Founder and President, Mercy Multiplied
Nashville, Tennessee

I'm grateful for Rob Ketterling as a friend, as a leader, and as an author. Rob challenges the way I think, and he helps me believe that the best is yet to come. If you're having a tough time trusting God, this book is for you. It will remind you that God hasn't given up on you!

Mark Batterson
New York Times **Best-Selling Author of** *The Circle Maker*
Lead Pastor of National Community Church
Washington, DC

My friend, Rob Ketterling, is truly one of the greatest leaders I know. I'm so thankful that he is sharing the wisdom God has given him in *Fix It!* This book illustrates the principles of responsibility in a way that is honest and refreshing. If you struggle to know what you should delegate, what you should keep on your plate, and what you should give to God, then this book is a must-read.

John Bevere
Author/Speaker
Cofounder, Messenger International
Colorado Springs, Colorado

Leaders often live under the pressure of an unattainable standard of perfection, which is why Pastor Rob's book, *Fix It!*, is an essential tool. Each chapter is packed with simple and profound strategies. Leaders are empowered to lead "with freedom, joy, and God's awesome power"!

Lisa Bevere
New York Times **Best-Selling Author**
Cofounder, Messenger International
Colorado Springs, Colorado

There is freedom that comes when you realize you shouldn't do everything! Rob Ketterling does a brilliant job of reminding us that there are some things you should do, some things that others should do, and some things that only God can to do. *Fix It!* offers valuable and refreshing insights on leadership, responsibility, and delegation that will encourage and inspire you to live and lead differently.

Randy Bezet
Lead Pastor, Bayside Community Church
Bradenton, Florida

Ministry can be messy because it includes people! But when we believe in people and do ministry *with* them and not *for* them, the body of Christ will become stronger as more people experience God's love and purpose for their lives. In *Fix It!*, my good friend, Rob Ketterling, does an incredible job presenting practical ways to grow as a leader, take responsibility when it's our turn, delegate when it's another's turn, and trust God for His provision and miracles when it's His turn.

Rick Bezet
Author and Lead Pastor at New Life Church of Arkansas
Conway, Arkansas

Problem solving is the essence of what leaders do. To leaders, problems are not a distraction, but opportunities for growth and improvement. Not every problem is the leader's responsibility to fix, yet many leaders desperately try to do what others should be doing, and they feel responsible even when only God can solve the problem. Pastor Rob Ketterling, out of his own experiences, helps us to determine what we should own, what others should be responsible for, and what should be totally turned over to God. Add to your leadership development and *Fix It!*

Doug Clay
General Superintendent at General Council of the Assemblies of God
Springfield, Missouri

"Let go and let God." We've all seen the bumper stickers, and it's good advice . . . sometimes. Yes, as Rob Ketterling will affirm in this book, there are times when we should leave demanding situations in God's hands. Yet other times we may "let go" too quickly. God has given each of us time and talents to use for Him. He has challenged us to train other people to do the work of the Kingdom. When we are too hasty in leaving to Him the things we could do personally or delegate to eager volunteers, we rob ourselves and others of valuable growth opportunities. As you implement Rob's suggestions for how to differentiate between "You," "Them," and "God," you will find your ministry's passion and purpose reenergized!

Herbert Cooper
Author of *But God Changes Everything*
Senior Pastor, People's Church
Oklahoma City, Oklahoma

How many times each week (or each day, or each hour) do you catch yourself saying, "I'll take care of that"? Before you say it again, you need to read *Fix It!* Rob Ketterling offers his sound and proven wisdom to help relieve you of much of the unnecessary weight you're carrying by entrusting it to someone else just as responsible. In doing so, your workload is reduced, and others get to experience the thrill of contributing their gifts to the Kingdom. And sometimes, all of you just stand back and watch God work His miracles to bless the work you're doing together. Read this book, do what Rob says, and see if you don't immediately find time and relief when you're not "taking care of that" so often.

Wilfredo "Choco" De Jesús
Senior Pastor, New Life Covenant Church
Chicago, Illinois

Whether in the marketplace or local church, organizational health is critical to success and sustainability. Intentional leadership is required, but with leader fatigue at an all-time high, many organizations are simply not healthy. Rob Ketterling's new book, *Fix It!*, is a must-read for every leader. The principles he lays out will help you learn the art of delegation from someone who had lacked it, then learned it, and now models it. This is a key component to your success as a leader today as well as the legacy you will leave tomorrow.

Lee Domingue
Founder of Kingdom Builders
Author of *Pearls of the King*
Associate Pastor at Church of the Highlands
Birmingham, Alabama

If we believe the weight of the world is on our shoulders, we'll be arrogant when things go well and crushed when they don't. Rob Ketterling shows us there's a better way. With biblical insights and wonderful stories, he helps us see how we can trust God to define the limits of the load we carry.

Craig Groeschel
Pastor of Life.Church and *New York Times* Best-Selling Author
Oklahoma City, Oklahoma

Rob Ketterling is so honest about the many mistakes he has made that you might wonder how he ever got to be such a well-respected and popular pastor. Yet therein lies one of his greatest lessons. In addition to the you/them/God breakdown he promotes, his willingness to confess to all the twists and turns he has had to maneuver in his ministry will challenge you to a greater level of perseverance in your own leadership. Many books offer worthwhile principles. But what makes Rob's lessons leap to life is how he shows the reader, "Before this principle worked for me, here's why it almost didn't!" As he shares his own journey of doubt and faith, fear and confidence, and tragedy and triumph, he will inspire you to set a more adventurous path for yourself.

Chris Hodges
Senior Pastor, Church of the Highlands
Birmingham, Alabama

When something breaks in today's world, everyone knows about it in a matter of minutes. Culture releases the bloodhounds to search out why it broke or what went wrong. In *Fix It!*, Rob Ketterling sagely guides us to the real heart of the matter . . . the who. Leaders carry the weight of the world on their shoulders, and Rob pulls no punches about the gravity of responsibility. I'm thankful Rob took the time to pen a well-balanced manifesto that's a strong reminder for us all to not give up on God because—even and *especially* when things go wrong—God doesn't give up on us.

Rob Hoskins
President of OneHope Inc.
Pompano Beach, Florida

Rob Ketterling is a devoted follower of Jesus and a committed builder of His Church. He has purposefully assembled biblical truths and personal experiences to strengthen and encourage every reader to live and lead with God's amazing power.

Brian Houston
Global Senior Pastor, Hillsong Church
Sydney, Australia

Rob Ketterling has a gift of telling stories, but his stories aren't just to entertain us. In *Fix It!*, he illustrates the principles of responsibility with humor and wisdom so we can delegate more effectively, rest more fully, and trust God more than ever.

John C. Maxwell
***New York Times* Best-Selling Author and Leadership Expert**

Most leaders are great at identifying what needs to be changed or fixed in their organization. The real problem comes when we think we can solve all the problems ourselves. Rob's book spoke directly to me as a "fixer," and I know it will help you lead with more clarity and efficiency in the days ahead. This is a must-read for any leader.

Dr. Todd Mullins
Senior Pastor, Christ Fellowship Church
Palm Beach Gardens, Florida

Rob is not just a long-time friend to me. He's been an example in my life of constantly striving to hear from God and do what's right. We have worked hard together and laughed hard together, and we've walked through some tough times together. So I'm excited to see him release this book because

I've watched him live its message. It gives us renewed life when we realize that not everything is on our shoulders to do, that God has put people in our lives to carry one another's burdens, and that we need to trust Him when we realize that a situation may be totally His to carry. There's life in this book because Rob's life is in it, and God has breathed on it. I know its message will refresh you and help you as it has me. Thanks, Rob, for obeying God and writing this book!

Dino Rizzo
Executive Director, Association of Related Churches
Associate Pastor, Church of the Highlands
Birmingham, Alabama

Fix It! addresses one of the most pivotal skills for succeeding in life and leadership: identifying where responsibility lies when it comes to problem solving. In my 30+ years of leading people, I've found if we want to see growth, we have to develop a healthy, balanced understanding of who is responsible for fixing a problem: us, someone else, or God. Rob provides a simple but powerful filter that can help simplify even complicated decisions so you can create solutions and move forward. I know this book will help you approach problems and decisions with a new perspective. I'm confident as you put the principles in this book into action, you'll experience greater momentum, peace, and confidence personally, and you'll be better positioned to accomplish all God has called you to do.

John Siebeling
Lead Pastor, The Life Church
Memphis, Tennessee

Rob Ketterling has clearly defined who is responsible for what. This seems like a simple task for leaders, but it's not . . . not at all. Most of us desperately try to do what others should be doing, and we still feel responsible when only God can solve our problem. Rob helps us know what goes in our bucket, what goes in other people's buckets, and what goes in God's bucket.

Greg Surratt
President, Association of Related Churches
Founding Pastor, Seacoast Church
Charleston, South Carolina

FIX IT!

WHOSE
PROBLEM
IS IT?

ROB KETTERLING

Copyright © 2018 by Rob Ketterling

All rights reserved. No part of this publication may be reproduced, stored in retrieval system, or transmitted in any form or by any means—electronic, mechanical, photocopy, recording, or otherwise—except for brief quotations in printed reviews, without the prior written permission of the publisher.

Unless otherwise noted the version of the Bible used in this book is the NIV.

THE HOLY BIBLE, NEW INTERNATIONAL VERSION®, NIV® Copyright © 1973, 1978, 1984, 2011 by Biblica, Inc.® Used by permission. All rights reserved worldwide.

Passages marked NLT are from the *Holy Bible*, New Living Translation, copyright © 1996, 2004, 2015 by Tyndale House Foundation. Used by permission of Tyndale House Publishers, Inc., Carol Stream, Illinois 60188. All rights reserved.

The anecdotes throughout this book are all true, although many names have been changed to ensure anonymity for the person(s) involved.

ISBN: 978-1-949837-00-1
Published by River Valley Resources
Printed in the United States

CONTENTS

This book is dedicated to everyone who steps up and fixes the problem and never gets the recognition.

You may not ever get the credit, but the solutions you find bring more than you can know! Thank you.

FOREWORD

You . . . Them . . . Him. That's this book in a nutshell.

It may sound simplistic, but it's not. The genius of this book is how Rob Ketterling targeted the problems all leaders face, deconstructed them, and wrote a book that will be a lifesaver for all who read it. This book is not just for leaders of churches, corporations, or organizations. The truths and concepts apply to all walks of life—including our homes.

I'm an organizational leader and consult with major organizations worldwide. This book challenges me to ask the diagnostic questions of *you, them, or Him?* More importantly, I'm a husband, father, father-in-law, and grandfather, and I can see how many of my relational challenges originated when I did not discern accurately the *you, them, Him* principle.

Of course, life is not always segmented neatly into clean categories. Sometimes it's you alone. Sometimes it's you and them. Sometimes it is you, them, and Him. My mathematician friends could calculate innumerable permutations and combinations of you, them, and Him . . . and that is the essence of this book. How we perceive and contextualize the situation, ourselves, others, and God determines each diagnosis, prescription, and outcome.

What I love about *Fix It!* is that Rob Ketterling doesn't offer philosophical paradigms around you, them, and Him. He unpacks this profound truth with personal and organizational examples. His total transparency, engaging ethos, and exceptional communication made me laugh out loud at times, and other times clouded my eyes with tears.

I found this book to be encouraging, instructional, and full of hope. I know Rob Ketterling well and am encouraged that he would unpack his life on this global stage so all can learn from his lifetime of experiences.

Sometimes it's *me*. Sometimes it's *them*. Sometimes it's *Him*. Often it is a combination. Knowing the distinctions in each situation you face can and will make all the difference in the world.

I love Rob Ketterling. I love this book. You too will love both.

Sam Chand
Leadership Consultant and author of *Leadership Pain*

CLEARING AWAY THE CONFUSION

Quite often, you often have to figure out on the fly how to fix a problem. It doesn't mean you haven't prepared; it just means something is in the way of your desired outcome, and you need to get past it, over it, or through it before you can accomplish your goal. Trust me when I say that I am a problem solver, that I'm a survivor, and that I believe you can learn to be one too!

Back in 1995 when we started River Valley Church in a school, I immediately began looking for a permanent home for us. As it always happens with new church startups, the people who attended often asked, "Pastor Rob, when are we getting our own building?" I told them again and again, mostly believing in faith, "I don't know, but I'm sure God has something wonderful for us."

I eventually found an empty field on the corner of a key intersection in Apple Valley, Minnesota, where four communities converge. It was close to town and appeared to be a prime location for the future. I often walked through the field and prayed,

"Lord, someday I'd love for You to let us build a church on this corner."

About four years into the life of our church, I drove to that familiar field early one morning, but this time it wasn't empty. A surveyor was staking out a foundation and trucks were unloading bulldozers. In Minnesota winters, it helps to have a vehicle that can handle the snow, so I was driving a four-wheel-drive Jeep Grand Cherokee. I didn't even stop to get out and look over the situation. Instead, I drove up to the man in the bulldozer, leaned out the window, and waved my arms to get his attention (in case driving my Jeep right up to him had escaped his notice). I yelled over the roar of his diesel engine, "Hey, what are you building?"

He yelled back, "An office warehouse."

I smiled and said at my highest decibel level, "I'm going to put my church here!"

He looked at me like I'd lost my mind, but he didn't say a word. He put the enormous machine in gear and started moving dirt.

As I drove away, I noticed a new sign in the lot with a phone number on it. I called and reached the leasing agent of the project. I asked him, "Do you have the warehouse you're building fully leased?"

He replied, "No, not yet."

I told him, "Great. I want to rent space from you for our church! When will it be ready?"

He paused for a second and then asked with more than a hint of skepticism, "Who puts a church in a warehouse?"

I replied, "It's being done in a lot of cities around the country." Another long pause told me he wasn't buying my explanation, so I continued, "If I can show you some places where churches are meeting in warehouses, will you rent me the space?"

A few days later, I picked him up, along with the owner of the building, and took them on a tour of a church in Minneapolis that meets in a warehouse. They were surprised and impressed. As we walked out, the owner asked, "How much money can you put down?"

I wasn't offering to buy the warehouse, so I was a little confused. I stammered, "What do you mean?" Before he answered, I blurted out, "I got nothing!"

He explained, "I'll need $110,000 for the buildout down payment and a deposit of $250,000."

I'm not sure what words came out of my mouth, but I'm certain my face screamed, "You've got to be kidding!"

He saw that I wasn't tracking, so he told me, "No problem. You can give me a letter of credit for the $250,000."

Being a shrewd negotiator, I asked, "What's a letter of credit?"

He smiled, "That's when someone who *has* money signs a letter promising to pay if the person who *doesn't have* money defaults on a debt."

I caught on quickly: "So . . . you don't really need the money. All you need is a letter from somebody with money, right?"

We drove back to Apple Valley and I dropped them off at his office. I got on the phone to see how in the world we could come up with the money and the letter of credit. After a few days, we had it . . . sort of. Becca and I started with all our retirement money, savings, the equity on our house, and the value of everything else we owned. It came out to about $100,000. In addition, my friend Dino Rizzo said that his church (Healing Place in Baton Rouge, Louisiana) would write a letter of credit for $150,000.

But there was a little problem. The denomination informed me that I couldn't take money out of my retirement account because I wasn't vested yet. I told them emphatically: "I need the money. If this church fails, I'll retire from our denomination. There won't be any problem then because I can take my money out to settle the debt." I was determined to solve this problem, and I was *all in*!

I visited the property almost every day as the warehouse was built and our space was finished. I envisioned thousands of people from the community coming to hear God's Word and maybe even joining our church, although at the time we were only 270 people. The process was moving along fairly well . . . until I got a call that the contractor (who had provided the lowest bid and whom I had hired over the owner's concerns about him) left town with $60,000, leaving behind an unfinished space. I now had to re-raise that money too. I also became the general contractor, and in case you don't know me very well, I'll let you in on a secret: I have absolutely zero experience or expertise in construction. None. Zip. Nada. On workdays, my dad used to let me read and study around our home because I was so bad with a hammer!

I tried to get all the plumbers, electricians, and other contractors to work in tandem, but the more directions I offered, the more confused they all became. I was gumming up the works and slowing things down even more! This was in June, with a huge delay staring me in the face, and the church was supposed to open in August. As days passed, my optimism eroded and even faint hope died as I realized I was a colossal failure as a contractor. Reality was incredibly difficult to take. One day I was so discouraged by the mounting problems that I sat in my office and thought, *I'm done. What can I do so that I'll be fired from the ministry but I won't lose my wife? Adultery? No, Becca would be gone. Drugs? No, I don't know anything about them. I'd probably overdose and die.*

After thinking long and hard, I came up with a brilliant plan: I was going to write down everything I didn't like about each person in the church, go to the liquor store and buy a bottle of vodka, get drunk for the first time in my life, and call all of them to tell them off! I was certain I'd get fired, but I'd keep Becca.

When I got home that afternoon, Becca could tell I was really depressed. She had never seen me like this, and she knew the source of the problem. That evening she secretly called everybody in the church who was supportive (even people on my list!) and asked them to meet at the warehouse the next night. She told them, "Rob needs us to be there to tell him we believe in him." The next day was another disaster at the warehouse, but that night Becca and I had scheduled a date. After dinner, she asked me to drive to the painfully unfinished warehouse. When we got there, I saw all the cars, and I got angry. I blurted out, "What's going on? What are all these people doing here at night? Are they vandalizing our building?"

Becca looked at me and said gently (okay, make that *firmly*), "Chill out, Rob."

We walked in, and as soon as we went through the door, dozens of people cheered for me. Instantly, I broke down and cried. Person after person said things like, "We believe in you, Pastor Rob. We're with you. We'll get into this building before too long." One of them said, "You're a lousy contractor, but you're a really good pastor." He paused a second and then added, "No offense." No offense taken. I can live with that.

It was a full year from the early morning when I drove my Jeep onto the grounds and waved down the guy driving the bulldozer until the day we opened the doors to the church in the warehouse. It was 2000, and our church was finally moving out of a school. No more early Sunday morning equipment setups and Sunday afternoon takedowns. I'm not sure who was more excited—me, or all the people who had worked so tirelessly for the past four years when we met in a school. The warehouse was in a perfect location.

To promote our grand opening (now pushed back to a Sunday in September, but finally set), I had a full-color tri-fold mailer designed and printed. We sent it out to 25,000 homes. We were ready . . . I thought. The final details of the buildout took longer than I thought, so timing was really tight, even with the delay. On the Thursday before the opening, the building inspector came to give us the final, official green light. After he looked at everything, he told me with a deadpan expression, "Your restrooms didn't pass. You can't open until they're fixed."

I was incredulous. (I shouldn't have been, but I was.) I barked, "That can't be! We're opening on Sunday. I've sent out 25,000 pieces of mail to invite people to come . . . this Sunday! We have to open! I have a mailer!"

He motioned for me to follow him into one of the restrooms. He showed me where the vent stopped above the ceiling instead of continuing all the way to the outside of the building. I said, "Okay, we'll get it fixed so you can come back tomorrow and sign off on us." He shook his head, so I insisted, "You don't understand—we're opening in three days! I sent out a mailer!"

With no hint of compassion or willingness to budge, he told me, "No, you're not. I can't come back until next week." He paused for a second, and his next words stabbed me in the heart: "In fact, I'm going to chain the doors closed because I'm pretty sure you'll try and still use the restrooms even though they failed inspection."

He was right, but I didn't tell him that. My mind raced to find a solution. I had it: "What if we put up porta-potties?"

He looked at me, thought for a second, and then said, "If you put up four for men and four for women, including two for the handicapped, you can open on Sunday."

That Sunday morning, eight portable toilets were lined up like soldiers on the front sidewalk of our church. Problem solved! Welcome to River Valley Church. Pay no attention to the porta-potties! Our attendance doubled that first day, and we've continually grown from there.

A lot of leaders are confused about who is responsible for a decision or an outcome that will fix the problem they face.

You, Them, and God

A lot of leaders are confused about who is responsible for a decision or an outcome that will fix the problem they face. The premise of this book is very simple. If we sit up and notice, we'll find three categories of responsibility:

- Some problems are up to *you* to fix;

- Other problems should be fixed by *them* (other people who report to, work for, or volunteer for you);

- And sooner or later, we'll all face problems only *God* can fix. (If you've picked up this book but you're not very religious, this is the category where you admit you need a miracle—which puts you pretty close to saying you need God to fix it!)

I learned to differentiate these responsibilities because of my disastrous experience as a general contractor (and through many similar subsequent problems). On that Thursday as I stood in front of the building inspector, I faced a problem I couldn't pass off to anyone else. I couldn't call a committee to meet and come up with a solution, I had no one to delegate it to, and I couldn't ignore it. Even praying in that moment wasn't changing the inspector's mind. It wasn't God's problem; it was mine. It was a "right now" problem, and it was all on me.

If I hadn't jumped in to resolve the issue, we would have had a colossal mess—and I'm not just talking about in the restrooms. Our church's reputation could have been destroyed the same day we opened our new doors the first time!

Over the years, however, I've learned the hard way that not every problem is mine to fix. If I don't delegate responsibility and authority to other people, I overload myself and I prevent them from growing and from bringing their gifts to the problem. Neither of those outcomes is productive!

And sometimes no matter how much I pray, plan, and prepare, and no matter how well I delegate to competent, faith-filled people, I occasionally face dilemmas that are far beyond me and the people around me. God is the only one who can solve those problems.

When I didn't understand these distinctions of responsibility, I carried far too much of the burden and I felt stuck in the mud of thinking I had to do everything all the time. I was continually frustrated with myself, with the people around me, and if I'm honest, with God for not making my life easier even though I was working so hard. I was often angry at people for not stepping up, but I hadn't been clear about what I expected them to do. I was too active and assumed too much responsibility, and I was too passive when I failed to hand responsibility to others. In those times when God was the only resource, I often frantically tried to do what only He could do, and I resented taking the blame when things didn't work out the way I hoped. It was a mess, but it was the only way I knew to lead a church.

As the fog began to clear, I realized my failure to distinguish who owned the problem created even bigger problems. I created tension on our team because they got mixed messages and clouded expectations; I created tension with my wife Becca and our two boys because I walked in the door frustrated almost every evening; I created tension in myself because I assumed everything was on me; and I created tension in my relationship with God because I wasn't sure what He was willing to do when I faced seemingly insurmountable difficulties. With my flawed perspective, I multiplied problems instead of solving them.

Does this description sound familiar? It may, but perhaps I've been a bit too abstract. When I had misplaced expectations about who shouldered the responsibility in each instance, my heart began to resent the people who didn't step up, and I resented God because He didn't make them step up. I spiraled down into self-pity, feeling sorry for myself because life was so unfair. As I lost the joy of living and leading, I made more bad decisions, which created more stress, leading to more resentment and self-pity. My biggest problem had become me and my downward spiral! Not a pretty picture . . . but an accurate one. If I hadn't finally corrected my perspective, there wouldn't have been many of "them" left in our church.

When I spoke on this topic at a pastors' conference, several people came up to me with wide eyes and similar comments:

- "Thank you so much for clarifying who's responsible! Now I have categories I can use."

- "I realize that if I do my part and enlist others to do their part, leading will go much better for me and our church."

- "I didn't realize there are three categories. I was sure everything was in my category!"

- "You're like Jethro and I'm Moses [referring to Exodus 18]. You've identified a leadership problem of me doing too much, and you've given me a solution to share responsibility with people who can get the job done—and grow in their faith while they're doing it."

- "Thank you for reminding me that I can trust God when there's nowhere else to turn. He's loving and powerful enough to handle any problem. I needed to hear that again."

- "You said that when only God can fix a problem, we don't know how or when He'll answer our prayers. I think I've been demanding that God come through on my terms. You helped me see that I need to trust Him for *His* answers."

One man took me aside and almost whispered, "Pastor Rob, I'm the opposite of you. I've avoided taking responsibility for the things I know God has given me to do. And the people around me have been ready to jump in, but I haven't let them. I've hoped God would somehow magically appear and fix everything . . . and I mean *everything*. God is a long way from being active in my life . . . because I'm the problem. Your talk has helped me see that I'm the one who needs to step up to the plate."

From my own experience and from the feedback of other pastors, I believe some of us desperately need to distinguish the three categories of responsibility or we're going to crater. From time to time, virtually all of us need to be reminded of what we're responsible for, what others are able to do, and what should be left for God.

We see this pattern clearly in the Bible. We could point to many instances, but let me mention just a couple. In the conquest of Canaan, Moses put Joshua in charge (Deuteronomy 31:7-8). Leading the people was his responsibility, but his soldiers fought, bled, and died to conquer the land. At Jericho (Joshua 6), the walls were high and strong. There, God gave Israel an opportunity for obedience and the dignity of participation, but when the walls fell without a shot being fired, there was no doubt who made it happen!

The Apostle Paul was commissioned by the leaders in Antioch for his first missionary journey and by the Jerusalem Council for the second one. Barnabas went with him to assist on the first journey, and Silas on the second, but Paul was the undisputed leader; it was on him. In every city where people came to faith, Paul appointed elders to lead the fledgling churches. When Paul walked out of the city, church responsibility was now on them. But in several instances, the only solution to a problem was the mighty hand of God. For example, the Lord changed Paul's planned itinerary and led him into Europe. At Philippi, Paul met Lydia who was moved by the message of the gospel and became the first convert on the continent. But God wasn't finished: Paul then trusted Him to deliver a servant girl who was tormented by evil spirits, although he and Silas were arrested and thrown into prison as a result. God then caused an earthquake to shake up the jailer (in several ways), and the two church leaders were soon released to keep spreading the good news of Jesus' love and forgiveness.

We could look at many more examples, but you've probably thought of others even as you read these paragraphs. The point is clear: God has called leaders to lead, to delegate, and to trust Him to do what only He can do. When we get this right, amazing things can happen!

Let me be clear about another important point. I'm not saying that the only time we trust God is when only He can fix a problem. The distinction is about responsibility, not trust. As leaders, we trust God to direct us, and we act according to His leading, love, and power. We also delegate to others and encourage them to trust God for the same kind of leading, love, and power. Paul explained our part and God's part to the Christians at Philippi: "Therefore, my dear friends, as you have always obeyed—not only in my presence, but now much more in my absence—continue to work out your salvation with fear and trembling, for it is God who works in you to will and to act in order to fulfill his good purpose" (Philippians 2:12-13).

We work, we serve, we labor, and we strive, but not for our own honor or in our own strength. We trust the Spirit of God to work in us, through us, and for us in everything we do.

Minutes and Moments

As you'll see as you read this book, understanding the three delineations of responsibility isn't intuitive to me. In fact, learning this lesson has been a long, slow, and sometimes tortuous process! Two concepts kick-started my understanding: Years ago, I heard someone say that company presidents and CEOs (and by extension, pastors) are really paid for the five percent of decisions no one else can make. All the decisions may be important, but the top few are crucial to the life and health of the company, organization, or church. This insight helped me realize I had to be ready for the five percent. The second concept was, in many ways, an implication of the five percent of decisions: it is learning to distinguish between minutes and moments. *Minutes* are the amount of time we log in on any responsibility; *moments* are the situations when we have to step up and make crucial decisions.

Minutes are the amount of time we log in on any responsibility; *moments* are the situations when we have to step up and make crucial decisions.

For a long time, I was all about minutes. My first job when I was in high school was working in the lot of a car dealership. I drove cars from the parking lot to be serviced or to be detailed for the new owners. I washed cars and ran errands . . . anything my boss wanted me to do. I think I made $3.75 an hour, and I was glad to get it. I also worked as a busboy at Lee's Bar-b-que. At the end of each shift, each of us got a free dinner. It was tasty, but not as sweet as the paycheck. A few years later, I got a job mowing the lawn of a huge corporation. Every weekend, I sat on a riding lawn mower and went back and forth over acres of grass—but by then I made $10 an hour. I thought I'd hit the big time! One summer I worked at Valley Fair Amusement Park as a games operator who guessed people's age and weight. I delivered pizzas for Domino's, and when I was 20, I had a job doing data entry for a law office. Maybe the strangest job I had was working for a plastic toy manufacturing company. All day every day, I stared at a plastic injection mold machine. If the machine jammed, I pushed a button and the foreman came over to fix it. I think that qualified as one of the top ten most boring jobs in the history of the world. In all of these roles, I was paid for the minutes I spent doing the work assigned to me. I clocked in and I clocked out, and I didn't get paid if I wasn't present for the entire time. At some point, I realized everyone at my level got paid the same hourly rate whether we were star performers or so mediocre that we barely stayed employed. Soon I began distinguishing between the company's minutes and my minutes—the time I spent on their clock vs. my own time at night and on the weekends. I endured their minutes, and I lived for my minutes.

Those jobs taught me how to count hours, minutes, hourly wage, weekly income, and the taxes taken out. (I hated that last part.) My value to the companies was in the minutes I logged, and each company's value to me was the money they paid me for those minutes. If I wanted to make more money, I needed to add more value to my minutes by being more skilled.

This isn't a difficult concept to grasp. When our oldest son Connor got his first job making pizzas, he came home the first day and asked, "Hey Dad, how do people get a pay raise?"

I asked him, "Well, son, how many people can do your job?"

He blurted out, "Anybody!"

I laughed, "Then you ain't getting a pay raise, son! If you can move up into roles where fewer people can do the job, you'll make more money."

His eyes widened, "Like working the cash register?"

"Probably," I said. "How many people do that job?"

"Only two."

I didn't have to say another word. He got it. He told me, "I'm going in tomorrow and ask to be trained to work the cash register."

A week later he came home and announced, "Dad, I've figured this out: some people are paid to use their bodies and hands, and some are paid to use their minds. I want to be paid for using my mind."

Connor was way ahead of me when I was his age; I was still slow to learn. When I became a pastor, I brought my perspective about minutes with me. I believed my value to the church was primarily in the time I invested in the tasks that had to be done—the more the better. I did everything. Because we had a portable church at first, every Saturday I went to rent a truck right before the rental company closed. To get the lowest cost, I wanted to sign the lease as near to their closing time as possible, so I often stood waiting with their employees as people who had rented trucks brought them back just before closing. In Minnesota's sub-zero winter temperatures, diesel can freeze, so I parked the truck in my driveway with the motor running all night. I parked my car behind the truck so no one could steal it during the night while it churned on and on. Early on Sunday morning, I drove to our storage facility, loaded all the canisters in the truck, drove to the school, unloaded them, and set up for the worship service and children's activities. I quickly changed into clean clothes and led the church service. After church, I packed up everything, loaded the truck, put the canisters in our storage facility, and took the truck back to the rental office.

I didn't even think about finding a better way to make all this happen. To be honest, I didn't want anybody to steal my thunder. I wore my frantic pace and exhaustion as a badge of honor, and I sure wasn't going to share it with anybody. I was logging my minutes!

My most important moment in the week was when I stood in front of our people to share a message from God's Word. At some point, it dawned on me that my sermons were suffering (and the people listening were suffering) because the minutes to accomplish routine tasks were crowding out my moments of preparation. I realized that if I gave only pretty good sermons, my friends would put up with them and encourage me, but newcomers to our church wouldn't. They were looking for something better. My friends would say, "Yeah, I know it wasn't Rob's best, but he was at the hospital for four hours yesterday visiting with Sarah's mother. He listened to her, sat with her, and prayed with her. And he's doing so much behind the scenes to set things up every week. His sermon wasn't very good, but he's doing the best he can." They were giving me permission to be measured by my minutes instead of my moments.

I had to make a radical switch: from measuring myself by minutes (doing things plenty of others could accomplish) to measuring myself by moments (the things only I could give to our church). Unlike all the jobs I'd had throughout my life, my role as a leader required me to reevaluate what was most important . . . and what was getting in the way. The most important things I needed to do were the things only I'm responsible for, like preaching, officiating at a funeral, handling a complex situation like a moral failure, responding to a tragedy, discerning God's vision of our future, meeting with the mayor and other city officials about our building, and fundraising. Other people could be responsible for the myriad of details to make the church run well . . . if I would let them. If only I could overcome my guilt of not logging lots of minutes, my critical moments would bring the greatest value to the church I'm called to lead.

When I ran around doing all kinds of tasks, I thought I was being a faithful servant, but I realized I serve best when I operate in my leadership gifts during the most critical moments in each day, each week, and each year. When I began operating more effectively in my moments, it opened a floodgate of growth for our church and outreach in our community. Previously, minutes had been supremely valuable, but now moments were at the top of the priority list. I'm not getting paid for all the minutes I put in each week; I'm being paid as a leader for the five percent of decisions that only I can make. I'm being paid for the moments only I can do. Those are the critical moments that open or close doors, pave new paths or lead to roadblocks, stimulate growth or make us stagnant. I need to be fully engaged and ready for those few decisions because if I manage my moments well, the people around me will contribute minutes, hours, and days of effectiveness.

All of us have to live in the tension between minutes and moments. We can't just show up for the five percent of the time when we have to make hard decisions! Most of us have seasons, like the first years of a church plant, when we need to spend more time in the mundane tasks that simply have to be done. But even then, we need a plan to recruit, enlist, place, and encourage people to take some responsibility. Even as our churches grow, we'll find time to roll up our sleeves and be involved in the nitty gritty of outreach, caring for the poor, and helping others in need.

I heard that during the busiest week of the year when his office sent out resources to thousands of people and churches, Pastor Charles Stanley would spend that week in the shipping department to help the people who serve there. He knows his most valuable moments are in leading InTouch Ministries, preaching, and teaching, but he hasn't forgotten that sometimes minutes matter just as much. I'm sure his minutes of rolling up his sleeves to work side-by-side with his staff members felt like significant moments to them. That's how leaders connect with their people, and that's how they build credibility and trust. Your minutes matter, but if you're the leader, your moments matter more! Learn to master those moments!

Your minutes matter, but if you're the leader, your moments matter more! Learn to master those moments!

My Hope for You

It's impossible for me to overstate how important it has been for me to grasp the differences in my responsibilities, the ones I need to delegate to others, and the ones only God can shoulder. It has lightened my load, made me a far better leader, enlisted many more people in building God's kingdom, and revealed the awesome power of God more than ever before.

You will see that this book has three parts: "It's on *You*," "It's Up to *Them*," and "Only *God*." Some of us will immediately identify with one of these more than the others, but I hope you'll read all three parts so you'll understand how they relate to each other. I want this book to give you hope and handles: hope that you can clearly delineate who is responsible for each task in your church, and handles on the decisions you need to make so that you live with freedom, joy, and God's awesome power.

At the end of this introduction, each chapter, and the conclusion, you'll find some questions to stimulate your thinking and help you apply the principles. Take your time to think and pray through them. There's no hurry. The Lord may want to speak to you as you reflect on the concepts and stories as you read. You can also use these questions as discussion starters for conversations with your leadership team as you study this book together.

Think about it:

1. What are some reasons leaders assume either too much or too little responsibility? What are predictable results of each error?

2. How does assuming too much responsibility often produce resentment, self-pity, more stress, bad decisions, and a spiral downward into more problems?

3. In your ministry, what's the difference between minutes and
    moments?

4. What percentage of your time is devoted to minutes, and how
    much is invested in moments? What, if anything, needs to
    change? What difference will it make?

5. What do you hope to get out of reading this book?

PART 1

IT'S ON *YOU*

CHAPTER 1

OUTSIDE THE BOX

Quite often, it falls on the leader to fix a problem, and many times we need more than a little shot of creativity. When the chips are down, we have to think outside the box.

At the first meeting of River Valley Church, thirteen people showed up. Only four of them weren't related to me or weren't promised a job at the church when we could afford them. Of those four, two never came back. It wasn't exactly the most auspicious start to a church, yet I immediately started looking for a school we could rent where we could meet.

I found two schools in Rosemount, Minnesota, that were possibilities. The first one had an open classroom setting: not many walls and just some bookcases as dividers between classes of students. As I walked through the building, I strolled past a row of bird cages holding cockatoos and parakeets, with bird poop spattered on the floor. I tried to envision a nursery of crying babies and toddlers running around without any walls to contain them. I thought of groups of children who didn't exactly need additional distractions to keep them from listening to a Bible story. And then I imagined telling visitors, "We're so glad to have you visit River Valley! I hope you were able to dodge the bird poop on your way in today." Option 1 was out.

Option 2 was Shannon Park Elementary School. It was perfect—a dream come true. The school was brand new. I asked if we could use the gym, and the principal responded, "Yes, you can do that."

I asked, "How many classrooms can we use?"

"None," was the instant reply.

"But we have to have classrooms for the nursery and the children's classes."

"Sorry, we can't let you have them. You can use the gym that divides into three spaces. That's all."

I had to think fast. I told him, "What if I use the teachers' lounge for the babies?" I unashamedly pulled the baby card on him. "You know we can't have babies in the hallway. That just wouldn't be right."

When I saw he was still hesitant, I looked him in the eye and said, "It would be heartless to leave the babies in the hall."

Finally, he agreed to let us use the teachers' lounge as our nursery—a victory for River Valley Church and infants everywhere! The gym could be divided into thirds, so we used the dividers to section off one third for children's church. The rest would be where we worshiped. The toddlers, of course, couldn't be in children's church, so we put them down a hallway with portable canisters forming a corral to keep them in.

In a remarkable display of the sinfulness of the human heart, the toddlers soon formed rebellious gangs. Four or five of them somehow decided to form a secret alliance, and with their combined strength, they pushed the heavy canisters enough so they could escape. I wondered why in the world parents of toddlers would let their kids stay in a makeshift area like this hall, but then I realized parents of toddlers are willing to leave their kids anywhere. They would have been okay with us putting them in the mechanical room and giving them wrenches as toys. (Not really, but if you've had a toddler you know I'm not that far off!)

Not long after we started, a tornado blew through the area one Saturday night and knocked out power to the school. The financial stability of new churches hangs by a thread, and losing a single offering can be devastating. We had to have church somewhere! I called the pastor of a church on the other side of town that still had power and asked if we could worship with them that Sunday morning. "The only thing I ask," I explained, "is that you let us take up a separate offering for the people from our church." He agreed, and we sent out word for everybody to go to the church across town. When we arrived, their bass player hadn't shown up, so our bass player joined their band for the day.

It gets stranger: That morning, the other pastor announced that he was resigning. After he spoke, he told his people, "If you don't make it as a church after I'm gone, River Valley looks like a really good place for you to go and join them in worship!"

Again and again, I had to find creative solutions to the problems we faced. Tornado knocks out your power? Go worship with a neighbor. Problem solved!

Tunnel Vision

As the old saying goes, "If all you have is a hammer, everything looks like a nail." But not everything is a nail. Problems come in all shapes and sizes. If we aren't thoughtful and innovative, we'll miss some golden opportunities to grow.

Here's an example. Someone once challenged me to connect
nine dots with only four straight lines without lifting my pen. He
assured me it was possible. See if you can do it. Don't turn the
page until you figure it out . . . or give up.

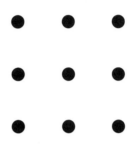

Early in our church's history, I needed to hire some staff
members, but we didn't have enough money to pay them. I went
to some key donors in the church and made a proposition: If they
would pay half a staff member's salary for a year, at the end of that
year we'd determine if the staff member's role had created significant growth in the church. If it did, the additional money from
new attenders would pay the other half of the salary; if it didn't,
we'd thank the person for his or her service and close the book on
that role . . . at least at that point. Several donors were happy to
fund half of the salary of new staff members. It was an awesome
solution to our need for more leadership.

Sometimes we have a need for a full-time staff member, but
either the church can't afford it or the person we want is only available part-time. Part-time is better than no time. Hire the person
you need and trust God to get a lot of work done in half the time.

Pastors often need to think creatively about space in their
buildings. They may want to rethink putting toddlers in an
area where they can escape and bull rush the congregation, but

learning to think with an open mind often has positive results. For instance, as we grew and space got tight, I realized that moving the speaker's platform to one corner enabled us to add about fifty seats. It was an easy way to provide places for more people.

A year and a half after we opened our doors, our band was established and pretty good, but one week our drummer couldn't make it. With our style of worship, we had to have a drummer. I called other churches to see if they would loan us their backup drummer, but nobody had one they were willing to share. By then it was late on Saturday night and I had to find a different solution. I drove to a local music store and walked into the area where drums were displayed. Three employees were standing around. I said, "Hey, I have a proposal for you. Who wants to make $100 tomorrow morning?"

They looked surprised, but they didn't blow me off. I continued, "Our church needs a drummer for our band tomorrow. The only requirements are to know how to play the drums and show up sober. If you need a smoke break that's fine, but being high or drunk isn't fine. That's it. Any of you interested?"

One guy looked at the others to see how they were reacting, and then he looked at me: "One hundred dollars to play at your church in the morning?"

"Yep. That's it."

"I'm in."

After getting his name and number, I called our worship leader and told him, "I've got a drummer for you. He's showing up tomorrow morning. Don't ask too many questions." The next morning, he came on time. He wasn't a Christian, but he played the drums and was sober. It worked for everybody.

Our task as leaders is to look for solutions outside the normal boundaries of our jobs. Some of them will work, and some won't, but none of the ones we don't try will work. Speaking of going outside normal boundaries, how did you do with the nine-dot puzzle? I finally figured out I needed to think outside the box (literally) to solve this one. Here's the result:

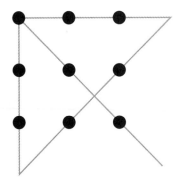

This solution showed me that I had lived with self-imposed limitations on the range of possible solutions to a wide array of difficulties . . . but no longer. Creative thinking gradually became normal for me.

Our task as leaders is to look for solutions outside the normal boundaries of our jobs. Some of them will work, and some won't, but none of the ones we don't try will work.

Some of us are suspicious of creativity because it seems to cause more problems than it solves. In a *Forbes* article called "The Rise of Creativity as a Key Quality in Modern Leadership," David Slocum describes the innate tension between creativity and leadership: "To speak of a creative leader, or manager, is for some a paradox: creativity is chaotic and unrestrained while leadership is orderly and controlling, and setting the two together makes for an uneasy, potentially volatile combination." Slocum traces the history of innovative modern leaders from Henry Ford to Peter Drucker, and he looks to the future:

> Returning to the words "creative" and "leadership" themselves, freighted as they are with history, offers some guidance. Together, they suggest bringing novel thinking to leadership challenges and at the same time deploying strategic prioritizing and decision-making to creative opportunities. Rather than antitheses, the words can convey a necessary balance and even symbiosis that support a sustainably successful creative business. No creative leader could ask for more.[1]

Creativity isn't a distraction or merely an add-on for leaders; it's essential if we're going to take our churches where God wants them to go. Just a quick glance at Jesus will show us He was very creative in problem solving. He told his disciples to go fishing to pay a tax bill (Matthew 17:24-27). He spat on the ground to create mud for a miraculous healing of a man's blindness (John 9:6-7). He fed a multitude with a few fish and loaves of bread (John 6:9-12). Where others saw limits, Jesus saw creative, miraculous solutions!

Collaboration vs. Isolation

It didn't take me very long in leadership to realize that there's a direct correlation between the time I spend with creative people and my level of creativity. I'm sure some people may be more creative when they're alone, but I don't know any of them. Even people far over on the scale toward introversion are stimulated and challenged by other artists, thinkers, and leaders.

I've known a lot of pastors who feel enormous pressure to be "the guy" who comes up with every detail of a brand new idea that will revolutionize their ministry—and every ministry around the world. Far more often, they would do better to take a good idea and make it great, or maybe take a great idea and adapt it to their situation.

For some reason, many leaders don't feel the freedom to be creative. I'm sure some of them tried to do something innovative in the past and failed, and it killed their creative spark. Or they tried to implement a new idea and the people around them thought they were nuts. They concluded that it's safer to keep doing the same things the same way, yet they end up with the same people . . . and maybe fewer of them. Many of us are afraid to push because we're convinced people expect us to be nice at all costs, and being nice means never making people feel the least bit uncomfortable.

I wasn't afraid to push when the principal told me we couldn't have any classrooms for our kids. People in business and education expect some push and pull from people who have an agenda, and I had an agenda: to find the best place for our church to launch and become a unified body that honors God by building His kingdom! Yeah, I pushed a little to make that happen.

When we've got problems and want to find a creative solution, we need to remember the story of Daniel and his friends (Daniel 1). The nation of Israel had been in trouble for a long time. The northern tribes had been defeated by the Assyrians, and now the Babylonian king, Nebuchadnezzar, led his army in a siege of Jerusalem. They destroyed the temple and took the gold items as loot, leaving many people dead in their wake. That was bad enough, but it got worse. The people were marched into exile, far from their home and their temple. In Babylon, Nebuchadnezzar ordered his chief of staff to round up the finest young men of Judah and train them for three years to serve the king. Imagine the situation for those young Jewish men: their city was in ruins, their nation devastated, and they were prisoners who were commanded to serve the man responsible for such carnage!

Nebuchadnezzar ordered his servants to provide the young men with the finest royal food and "teach them the language and literature of the Babylonians" (Daniel 1:4). The king wanted to thoroughly indoctrinate them so they became indistinguishable from his most loyal servants. But Daniel and his three friends were faithful to God and His dietary laws, and they weren't willing to eat the king's spread. They could either cave in and eat or refuse and die . . . or they could find a creative solution. Daniel talked to the chief steward and made him an offer: "Please test your servants for ten days: Give us nothing but vegetables to eat and water to drink. Then compare our appearance with that of the young men who eat the royal food, and treat your servants in accordance with what you see" (Daniel 1:12-13).

When the ten days were over, Daniel and his friends were healthier and stronger than the men who ate the king's food. The narrator describes the scene:

> To these four young men God gave knowledge and understanding of all kinds of literature and learning. And Daniel could understand visions and dreams of all

kinds. At the end of the time set by the king to bring them into his service, the chief official presented them to Nebuchadnezzar. The king talked with them, and he found none equal to Daniel, Hananiah, Mishael and Azariah; so they entered the king's service. In every matter of wisdom and understanding about which the king questioned them, he found them ten times better than all the magicians and enchanters in his whole kingdom (Daniel 1:17-20).

Daniel could have thought that God had abandoned him and his friends, so they would have nothing to lose by eating the king's dishes, or he could have presumed it was God's will for them to eat it since He had allowed them to be captured. But in the heat of the moment, Daniel kept his head and looked for a solution that was far outside the box. The risk, though, wasn't his alone. When Daniel made his proposal, the official in charge told him, "I am afraid of my lord the king, who has assigned your food and drink. Why should he see you looking worse than the other young men your age? The king would then have my head because of you" (Daniel 1:10). Daniel was asking him to risk his life to participate in his plan. In a similar way, but to a far lesser extent, when I asked the principal to bend the rules and let us use the teachers' lounge, he was putting himself at risk with the school district. It was worth the risk for both of us. We launched our church with his hesitant okay, and our church became an asset to the community. He looked good for agreeing to let us meet there, but it took courageous creativity!

Works of Art

Creative solutions are like works of art. The creators are vulnerable to the whims of the critics. When we display a painting or a sculpture, or present a novel solution to a problem, and the critics howl in response, it sure doesn't feel like they're making an objective statement about the art. It feels intensely personal—like they're stabbing us in the heart! Whether they say it or we assume it, the message we hear isn't "It's bad," but "You're bad!" It's very difficult to hear such comments without being crushed by them, but that's the task of every artist who has a show and every leader who tries to implement a fresh idea.

Most creative people live on the edge. I've told some musicians and artists, "That's pretty good." I might as well have said, "You're a total loser, and you'll never amount to anything!" Without a glowing review and angels singing backup to my affirmation, some artistic people can go to a very dark place and get deeply depressed.

Critics are judges who give a negative verdict, so we need to remember that we've been in the only courtroom that matters, and we've been declared not guilty by the Judge of all.

Critics are judges who give a negative verdict, so we need to remember that we've been in the only courtroom that matters, and we've been declared not guilty by the Judge of all—not based on our performance, but because Jesus took the guilt of our sin and paid it all. The world's critics are only clanging cymbals in contrast with the loving and lingering affirmation, "You are my beloved son or daughter, in whom I'm well pleased." God is pleased with us, not because we're perfect, but because we belong to Him. He has paid the ultimate price to ransom us, buy us back, and make us His own.

Scripture reminds us that Jesus "endured the cross, scorning its shame." What motivated such a sacrificial action? He did it "for the joy set before him" (Hebrews 12:1-3). What was "the joy set before" Jesus when He suffered and died that horrible death on the cross? It was having you and me as His own. We are His reward, we are His joy, we are what matters to Him. When we get a glimpse of the fullness of joy Jesus has in us, our hearts will melt, and His love will take the sting out of others' criticisms. We will see that His opinion is the only one that really matters.

From first to last, God has rescued us by His grace, empowered us by His Spirit, given us an incredible status as His children, and imparted the greatest purpose the world has ever known. In all of this, we need to see ourselves the way He sees us. In His great love and grace, He has "created us anew" and now considers you and me His works of art, His masterpieces (Ephesians 2:8-10 NLT).

When we become more secure in our identity as God's dearly beloved children, we're not as defensive, and we welcome help from others. When one of our ideas bombs and we're tempted to isolate, instead we can turn to people around us and ask, "What am I missing? What do you see that I don't see? Help me out. I'm listening."

We're foolish if we think creative ideas aren't going to get some pushback. It's going to happen, so get ready for it. But it hurts worse if it comes from people we respect and trust. Even then (especially then) we need to realize they're telling us what they think we need to hear, not to harm us but to help us. "Wounds from a friend can be trusted, but an enemy multiplies kisses" (Proverbs 27:6).

I've learned to formulate my response to criticism instead of just reacting—which, I admit, never works out very well. If I take time to think, I can say, "Here's what I was thinking . . . Here's what I thought would happen . . . Here's what we'll do next time so we'll have a better outcome . . ."

Too Far Outside the Box

Occasionally, our creativity can get us into trouble. Not long after our church began, Becca and I pledged $30,000 over three years toward the church's building fund. To raise the money, I started an inflatable games business—I was the king of bounce houses and giant inflatable slides! I was also the pastor of a growing church plant, and I had a young family, but in every spare minute, I ran all over town hauling and setting up inflatables for kids' birthday parties and other community events.

You need to know that I'm mechanically challenged. Some men can fix any engine in the blink of an eye; I'm more likely to put out someone's eye when I work on one. Again and again, I found ways to damage the equipment. I learned something very important in that business: when an inflatable game doesn't hold air, the kids aren't happy, and then the parents aren't happy. At the end of the three years, I had expected to make $40,000, so I'd have $10,000 for our family after meeting our pledge. I came up a little short. My business lost $20,000. I had to cash in my IRA and pay the penalty so we could make our building pledge. Starting the business was a creative idea, but it was too far outside the box of my skill set.

On the evening we closed the books on the business and paid our pledge, Becca and I sat down at dinner. I told her, "I'm so sorry I lost so much money. It was a disaster."

She looked me in the eyes and told me, "Rob, you were trying to move our family forward and make our church building pledge. I'm not blaming you for trying."

Instantly, I replied, "Honey, I love you! I'd marry you again right now!" I thank God I married a woman willing to let me lead outside the box!

Cultivate the Habit

Some people are more naturally creative, but all of us can improve our level of creativity. We can cultivate the habit of being bold and innovative, and we'll get better every time we make an attempt. Not all of our ideas will work, but we can learn from every instance.

When I was a young pastor, I couldn't stand listening to my sermons. I hated the sound of my voice, and I was sure what I'd said was unutterably elementary and maybe even stupid. After a while, however, I developed more confidence, and I began to realize the importance of developing my craft. Today I'm not shocked or ashamed when I realize I could have done better because I'm convinced I'll actually do better the next time I try it. Confidence in the future gives me the courage to be honest about today's mistakes. You and I will get better over time!

I have a principle that I call "The First Pancake," and I discovered this principle because I love to make pancakes for my family. (This is going somewhere, trust me!) I mix the batter and get all the extra ingredients ready for whoever wants to doctor up their stack. When the griddle gets hot, I put on the first pancake. The first one is okay, but the second one is better. Soon the griddle and the cook are in sync, and the rest of the pancakes are perfect. Thankfully, the first one is on the bottom of the stack and the best ones are on the top. If we don't get to the bottom while we're eating them, that's just fine.

Here's the point: you have to make the first pancake. It won't be your best, but you have to start the process. You won't get to the third or fifth or twentieth until you cook the first one. In every problem leaders face, they need to take a shot and see what happens. It almost certainly won't be perfect, but they'll learn how to do it better the next time, and the next, and the next. Once you get in sync, watch out! Perfect solutions and perfect pancakes!

You have to make the first pancake. It won't be your best, but you have to start the process. You won't get to the third or fifth or twentieth until you cook the first one.

As leaders, we can't push the responsibility of finding creative solutions on everybody else while we play it safe. It's up to us to set the tone of the church, to create a can-do, let's-go-for-it mentality, and trust God to produce extraordinary results. Creativity always involves risks. Yes, we might fail. Yes, we'll almost certainly be criticized even if it goes well. But if we remain in a shell of safety, we won't have the sheer joy of seeing people's eyes light up and their lives changed by a fresh and innovative idea, process, or program.

Timidity keeps us perpetually stuck in the problem while we dabble around the edges. We need to think outside the box and encourage others to think that way too. Then we'll find solutions that challenge us to trust God for bigger things, thrill us with the risks, and inspire us to pray more than ever. It's wise to think it through and consider contingencies, but at some point, it's time to step out and take a leap of faith. We won't see results until we do.

The people around us aren't responsible to make us creative, and we don't wait for God to miraculously intervene and give us solutions we were too afraid to try. It's on me; it's on you. You'll know you're ready to take the leap just like you know when you're ready to jump into a swimming pool of really cold water. You may stand on the side and count, "One, two, three, jump!" but your feet don't move. You try it again, but you're still immobile. Yet something in you says, "Okay, no more false starts. This is it." You take the leap, and it's done. This is the resolve you need to jump into a problem and find a creative solution. As a leader you say, "Okay, no more hesitations, no more analysis, no more fear. It's time!" And you find the courage to jump.

As you've read this chapter, perhaps the Holy Spirit has nudged you to remind you that you've been too passive about a particular problem. You've felt stuck and confused, and maybe you were afraid of what people would say if you took a bold step and fell flat on your face. As you take this step and learn from success and failure, the Lord may show you other areas where you haven't been as creative and courageous as you need to be. In each one, listen to the Lord, trust Him to give you a solution, and take the plunge. You're a leader. This is on you.

As creativity becomes a habit, people will ask, "How do you come up with so many great ideas?" You can say, "I'm on the sixth pancake."

Think about it:

1. What are some of the most common difficulties pastors face in their roles?

2. Which of these has been a particular challenge for you? How have you responded to it?

3. Why is collaboration important but threatening when leaders are looking for creative solutions?

4. How is creativity in leadership like art?

5. What are some ways we can tell if we're still in the courtroom of public opinion or if we're sure the verdict that matters is already in?

6. Why is it important to formulate our response to criticism instead of simply reacting?

7. Which pancake are you on? Explain your answer.

CHAPTER 2

IN A CRISIS

Like most portable churches in their early years, River Valley didn't have a permanent sign on the highway to remind people where we met. Instead, we invested in about half a dozen high-quality signs we would put out each week at the intersections of major roads near our church to guide people to our doors. Our signs were top of the line, three feet by four feet, A-frame heavy plastic with bright, clear vinyl graphics. They even had little handles on the top. They folded up very neatly and slid perfectly into a slot in one of the storage canisters. We paid real money for them. Nothing but class when it came to our signs.

Our setup team knew exactly where each one went so the arrows pointed in the right directions down the streets. One Sunday at the end of the service, a couple of the takedown guys (my brother Ryan and his friend Joe, two young guys to whom we gave the exalted title of "Site Coordinators") walked up to me with puzzled expressions on their faces. Ryan said, "Pastor Rob, we don't know what's going on, but several of our signs are missing." He paused a second and then asked, "Did . . . did you pick them up?"

I blurted out, "No, I didn't pick them up. What do you mean 'missing'?"

"Gone. Vanished. Not where we put them." (I guess he thought my question needed three answers.)

"How many of them?"

"Half of them. Three." (Now only two answers to my question. He must have thought I was catching on.)

I was sweating every dollar we spent, and these were expensive signs. I didn't want to buy even an extra roll of duct tape, and now they were telling me three of our first-class, very expensive signs were missing. They simply had to be replaced. No choice there.

It took two weeks for the company to make us three more signs. We made do with three in the meantime, and it's a wonder anyone found us without good signage! When the new signs were ready, we proudly put them out on the streets. But after the service, the guys came to me with a pained look on their faces. "Pastor Rob, you won't believe this . . ."

"Oh no, don't tell me."

"Yeah, another three signs. MIA."

I defiantly told them, "That does it! We can't put up with being vandalized like this!" I called the police and told the desk sergeant, "Someone is stealing the signs we put at intersections to direct people to our church."

With a completely dispassionate voice, the sergeant replied, "No one is stealing your signs. We're taking them."

I'm not sure exactly what I said next, but it was something like, "What? Why in the world are you doing that?"

He didn't miss a beat: "Because it's against the law."

I resisted the urge to shout, and calmly replied, "What are you talking about? Real estate companies put up their yard signs all over town!"

"Yes," he said slowly and deliberately, like he was talking to a small child, "but they have permission from the city for yard signs. Churches don't."

I took a deep breath and tried another angle. "Sir, we've been putting signs out for several years. I don't know what happened that you're picking them up now."

"Someone called in a complaint." He paused for a second, and then explained, "We don't really want to pick up your signs, but since someone filed a complaint, we have to."

The noble motives of the police department didn't calm me down or solve the problem. Okay, we had broken the law. I wondered if their next step was to come to our church, cuff me, and haul me away in the middle of a sermon. I asked, "What's the penalty for this?"

"We take your signs."

"That's it?" I was surprised. "There's no fine or imprisonment?" (I didn't really say the last word, but I thought it.) "Will this go on my record?" I wanted to ask if they were going to put my picture up at the post office.

"No, nothing like that. We just take your signs."

Instantly, the game changed. I thanked the sergeant and hung up. The setup guys had been listening to my side of the conversation. They were happy to hear me explain that they wouldn't have to visit the county jail to get instructions for next week's service. I told them, "Go to the sign company tomorrow and order a hundred foam board signs with metal stakes. They're cheap, and it won't matter if the police take them every week."

The guys asked, "So . . . we're going to keep putting signs out every week?"

"Absolutely. In fact, I want someone to be a scout. When the police take one of our signs down, wait until he drives out of sight and put another one in its place. And let's pick up the signs as soon as the last service starts so the police don't have a chance to get them during that service."

Then I had another idea: we owned a 24-foot truck to haul our canisters to and from storage each week, and the truck had blank sides. We had the sides of the truck painted with all the information about our church—including directions. After we unloaded every Sunday morning, we parked the truck at the most visible intersection near where we met. It was big, it was beautiful, and the police couldn't take it away because it wasn't by any stretch of the imagination a "yard sign."

Good leaders plan effectively, but they also react to sudden problems with clarity and boldness.

Planning and Reacting

Good leaders plan effectively, but they also react to sudden problems with clarity and boldness. We had carefully planned how we would point people to our church, and we spent lots of money on those beautiful plastic A-frame signs. But when we faced a minor crisis, we had to quickly come up with Plan B (and C).

When I called the police to report the theft of our signs, I got an answer that was completely unexpected. At that moment, my mind kicked into gear to find an immediate solution. I didn't just assume it was God's will that we couldn't have signs, and I was willing to absorb the cost of the cheap signs and the paint job on the truck to fix the problem.

Many leaders are gifted planners, but they are so wedded to their carefully constructed plans that they aren't flexible enough when the plans hit a snag. I'm not pitting planning and reacting against each other—we need to do both very well, and both of them are the leader's responsibility. We certainly involve others so they own their part of the planning process, but all of it is our part. As the plan is implemented, it's also our part to solve the unexpected problems that inevitably arise.

We can make one of two errors when a problem suddenly surfaces: we become paralyzed, or we act impulsively. Neither of those is effective leadership. Some people shut down in even a minor crisis. They feel devastated because the plan didn't work as they hoped. Their minds are clouded by a fog of fear and uncertainty. They may not be able to think at all, or they may become immersed in detailed analysis in an attempt to get control of the situation. Analysis is certainly necessary to *find* a solution, but not to *avoid* taking steps toward a solution. Fear can also drive leaders to the opposite extreme. The adrenaline they feel compels them to make a decision—any decision—without much thought about the wisdom of the choice or its consequences.

When our signs went missing, it was more than an annoyance. Most young churches can't afford prime real estate and are tucked into neighborhood schools or office buildings. Without our signs, people couldn't easily find River Valley Church! Our signs were the first greeters, the initial touch newcomers would experience. That's why we paid an arm and a leg for them. And remember, no one had heard of Siri yet. This was before the wide use of cellphones and apps that told exactly how to get from one place to another. Our signs were much-needed breadcrumbs to lead people to us. When they were missing, we had to find a solution and find it fast!

Every plan hits roadblocks and unexpected twists and turns. Leaders may take weeks to craft a plan, but they usually have only a short time—perhaps minutes or hours—to react to a problem. My advice is to plan well, but when problems inevitably happen, don't panic. Some of us are more on edge than others, but all of us can learn to stop for a second, look at the situation objectively, consider some options, determine the probable outcomes of each choice, make the best decision at the moment, and take action. We often realize later we could have made a better decision if we'd had more information, but we must act on what we know in the short window of time we have.

A lot of pastors I know put themselves in one of two categories: leaders who plan, or leaders who prefer to go with the flow. Each group is proud of its strengths. Planners can show you a hundred-page plan with spreadsheets, diagrams, and a PowerPoint. Before anyone asks a question, they already have the answer. But they may not be very nimble when things go wrong, and they don't respond well to pop-up problems. Other leaders think planning is a waste of time. They're "intuitive" on the Myers-Briggs personality test, and they assume that gives them permission to lead by the seat of their pants. They may have been fantastic fighter pilots in World War II when it was one intrepid man against the enemy, but their people need more than the leader's hunches to guide them.

If you don't plan well, the pop-up problems will accumulate like popcorn in the machine at the theatre! You won't
have time to solve each problem because there will be far
too many others to address.

Great leaders lean into their strengths, but they realize they
must cover both bases: plan effectively so they and their teams
know where they're going, and develop the presence of mind to
react in the moment when a crisis happens. Both are essential.

If you don't plan well, the pop-up problems will accumulate
like popcorn in the machine at the theatre! You won't have time
to solve each problem because there will be far too many others
to address. Your people will be frustrated, and you'll lose their
respect because you're running around trying to fix things they
know could have been solved earlier—or avoided completely—
by good planning. They'll wonder if you're worth following.

Some leaders insist, "If I plan too much, I'm leaving God out
of the process." That's often a smoke screen for laziness. Almost
always, those who have a comprehensive plan know they need
God's intervention to make it happen, and they realize they need
to leave plenty of margin for God to work in and through the
unexpected opportunities and difficulties. Planning is a valuable
roadmap, but when it becomes necessary, God can redirect us
and we can redirect our teams.

I think church plants are magnets for the unexpected. Almost
anything can happen, and it often does. We might plan to have a
family outreach with a bounce house for the kids, but when we

plug it in to inflate it, the circuit blows. If that happened to me, I would have no idea how to fix the blown circuit. I'd have one of two solutions: either quickly find somebody who knows something about electrical wiring or check every outlet on the building to find one that's still working. If we need to move the bounce house closer to the hot tub where we're going to baptize people, the kids might accidentally find their way into the water, but as long as everybody is safe and having fun, who cares? The plan to engage families in the community of faith was a really good one, but the blown circuit would force an audible. No matter what, we'd find a way to make it work.

On the other side of the continuum, some leaders are completely thrown off balance when the unexpected occurs. They might get angry at someone who should have prevented the problem, at themselves, or maybe at God. They may deny there's a problem and attempt to minimize it by saying, "It's no big deal," when everybody on the team knows it is. They might excuse the people responsible: "He couldn't help it." Any of these inadequate reactions erodes trust in the leader and becomes a slow leak that deflates everyone on the team. Gradually, people find other places to serve because they don't want to invest their lives with a leader who can't be honest about pop-up problems and find ways to solve them.

In a *Harvard Business Review* article, "How a Good Leader Reacts to a Crisis," John Baldoni contrasts the responses of the mayors of New York and Newark to devastating snowstorms. One of his tips for good leaders is to "demonstrate control":

> When things are happening quickly, no one may have control, but a leader can assume control. That is, you do

not control the disaster—be it man-made or natural—
but you can control the response. A leader puts himself
into the action and brings the people and resources to
bear. Think of Red Adair, who made a name for himself
putting out oil fires that no one else could. A raging blaze
may seem uncontrollable but Adair knew [he] could control the way it was extinguished.[2]

When leaders demonstrate control of themselves in a situation that's out of control, they think more clearly, act with more
confidence, and inspire their people to dive in and help solve the
problem. Even when problems arise that aren't your fault, a good
leader will take the responsibility to fix them.

In the Moment

As Moses led God's people out of Egypt to the Promised
Land, he and they saw God do amazing things. It began when
God had rescued the people from slavery through a series of
plagues on Egypt. God then miraculously saved them from certain annihilation by the pharaoh's army as they stood trapped on
the banks of the Red Sea. God gave Moses the Law on Mt. Sinai,
and He gave them the promise of forgiveness through the sacri-
fices in the tabernacle. He directed them by a pillar of fire and a
cloud of smoke. He gave them manna and quail out of the sky and
provided water out of the rocks. In spite of all these evidences of
God's presence, they complained. Over and over again, they told
Moses how unhappy they were with God and him.

At a place called Meribah, they again whined that they were
thirsty. This time God told Moses, "Take the staff, and you and
your brother Aaron gather the assembly together. Speak to that

rock before their eyes and it will pour out its water. You will bring water out of the rock for the community so they and their livestock can drink" (Numbers 20:8).

This was yet another pop-up problem on the way to see God fulfill the promise of a new life in a new land. Moses had been incredibly patient for four decades, but this time, he blew it:

> So Moses took the staff from the Lord's presence, just as he commanded him. He and Aaron gathered the assembly together in front of the rock and Moses said to them, "Listen, you rebels, must we bring you water out of this rock?" Then Moses raised his arm and struck the rock twice with his staff. Water gushed out, and the community and their livestock drank.
>
> But the Lord said to Moses and Aaron, "Because you did not trust in me enough to honor me as holy in the sight of the Israelites, you will not bring this community into the land I give them" (Numbers 20:9-12).

This failure was costly to Moses. He lost credibility, he lost self-respect, and he lost the opportunity to enter the Promised Land. When we're in similar situations, it's easy to become frustrated and react in anger like Moses. When this happens to me, I try to stop everything and step into the problem. I become totally focused and mentally alive. I block everything but the problem out of my mind: it's like I'm driving and I turn off the radio because I don't want the background noise to distract me. To use another comparison, I feel like I'm driving in an unfamiliar part of town and I come to an intersection where three roads converge. I don't make a snap decision; I quickly scan all the signs and take in all the available information, and then I intuitively ask myself "what ifs" and "what abouts." Very quickly, I eliminate a lot of options, and I can choose between the few remaining.

In the moment of a crisis, I go through my internal calculations very quickly, and then I can take charge of the situation and give clear directions to everyone involved. I've learned to stop, take a deep breath, and ask three questions in the first moments of a crisis, large or small:

- What is true right now?
- What are the options?
- Which option has the best chance of success?

Some people instinctively use this process, but anyone can learn it. Even those who are more methodical can follow this pattern of problem solving. They can begin by noticing their tendency to go brain dead or panic (or both) and stop to regroup. They can then do a quick evaluation of the situation, consider the options, make a decision, and take action. Like any acquired skill, it takes practice, but I don't think any of us have a shortage of pop-up problems that form the training ground for us to become skilled in this process.

What is true right now?
What are the options?
Which option has the best chance of success?

One of the biggest mistakes we can make is to catastrophize, thinking the situation is hopeless and it's the end of the world. Some people jump there first. If you don't think you can remember the three questions, write them on a business card and put them in your wallet or purse. I guarantee you that it won't be long before you need them!

Depending on the situation, I often ask the people around me the three questions. This has three benefits: I get their shared wisdom, they feel included in the process right now, and I'm training them to think this way when they face crises.

Leaders can't wait until they have every question completely answered before they make a decision and move forward. Quite often, we make our best decision (really, our best guess), and take a step or two. At any point, we may get more information and then make a course correction. As long as we're moving forward, we can adapt our solution so it's clearer, stronger, and more effective. If you assume it's others' responsibility to solve the problem or God's responsibility to magically make the problem go away, you abdicate your God-given role of leadership. Staying stuck doesn't produce good results, and it's a lousy model for your people. Cultivate the leadership habits of clear thinking and bold action, and be willing to adapt along the way.

In the heat of the moment, titles mean almost nothing. If the house is burning, you don't have a conversation about egalitarian or complementarian roles in a marriage. You give orders and get everybody out alive! At the church, when a crisis arises, I look at the people around me and immediately give directions to whoever is nearby. I may ask my executive pastor to do something very simple and mundane, but it must be done right now! In the crisis, there's no rank and no privilege. All that matters is solving the problem.

Immediately after the crisis is over and the adrenaline subsides, it's time to apologize, give grace, and be a cheerleader:

- **Apologize:** I may realize that I was pretty short in my directions to one of my executive pastors, so I tell him, "I'm sorry for being so abrupt when I spoke to you. I want to assure you I was intense, but I wasn't (and I'm not) angry at all. Are we good?" (And I may need to apologize to everyone who was within earshot of me.) I also apologize to anyone who had an idea I shot down, but later realized was better than mine. I might say, "Naomi, you were right. I'm sorry for not following your suggestion. It would have gone better if I had." (And you better believe I'll listen to Naomi more closely next time!)

- **Give grace:** One of the most common responses during and after a crisis is blame-shifting. Some people blame everybody but themselves, even if they were clearly at fault, but sensitive people often absorb blame that isn't theirs to own. If you have two or more people on your team, you almost certainly have both kinds! To dissolve the cloud of blame, offer a lot of grace. You might say, "Man, that was hairy, wasn't it? But God gave us grace to fix it. We didn't do it perfectly, but that's fine. We learned some lessons, and we worked as a team."

- **Be a cheerleader:** The people involved need to know you believe in them, and words of affirmation mean a lot. You can speak to the team: "Each of you played a big part in resolving this problem. I don't know what we would have done without you. I'm so glad you're on our team!" And you can speak to individuals in the meeting or one-on-one to be more specific about how much you appreciate each person's contribution.

As the dust settles, it's not yet time to have any kind of detailed analysis about the crisis. People who were with you need two things: comfort and a nap. You need to stay focused long enough to apologize, give grace, and be a cheerleader—those are the elements of comfort—and then take a break. A few days later, gather the team to debrief. You know the drill: How did it happen? What did we miss? What went right? How can we do better next time? What lessons did we learn? Depending on the crisis, this analysis may take minutes, hours, or even a day.

Some crises are relatively minor, like the circuit blowing when you plug in the bounce house, but others are far more serious.

Close to Panic

Our family went with a group of twenty from our church to Beijing, China, on a mission trip for a cultural experience and to deliver humanitarian aid. Back in the states, people were celebrating Thanksgiving Day, and we wanted to acknowledge the holiday. We couldn't find any roast turkey and dressing, so we had the next best thing: Beijing duck. In China, a gracious host always serves a lot more food than the guests can eat, and the restaurant obviously decided I needed to be a gracious host. After we had eaten until we almost popped, we still had platters full of food. We asked the waitress to box up the leftovers so we could take them to homeless people in the city.

To keep from looking like a mob of Americans invading a Chinese neighborhood, we split up into two groups. Becca and I went with one group, and our sons Connor and Logan went with the young adult crowd. We planned to meet in our hotel lobby two hours later. Our group gave out our food and got back first. A little later, a second group came in, but it wasn't all of them because some had separated and gone their own way. When the leader of the second group came in, he asked me, "Where's Logan?" I'm sure the expression on my face didn't communicate calm assurance, so he raised his voice a bit: "I thought he was with you!"

I told him, "No, he wasn't with us! He went with you!"

He said sadly, "Pastor Rob, I think he's lost."

It was a parent's worst nightmare. We had just come from seedy back alleys where people hid from the authorities and tried to squeeze out a living on scraps and handouts. Logan was an eight-year-old American blond boy. We'd heard stories of kidnapped American kids being sold on the black market. Horrible images shattered our composure. Becca and I both kicked into high gear, but we had very different reactions. Instantly, Becca convulsed in panic and fear. Sounds came out of her mouth, but they weren't real words. I jumped into my crisis management mode. Intuitively, I thought, *I'm Dad. I have to solve this right now!* My mind raced through my three questions. It took only seconds to arrive at an instant analysis, the options, and a plan. We needed everyone in that part of the city to know what Logan looked like, so I grabbed Becca and told her, "You have a picture of Logan. Take it to the front desk right now. Have them make copies we can distribute, and have them send a copy to the police." She started running to the front desk as she fumbled in her purse for the picture.

I told the group that had just come back, "I want you to retrace every step you took, every alley you went into, and see if you can find him!" They ran out like they'd been shot from a gun.

I turned to my team and said, "Pair up and go out into every alley where you think there might be homeless people. Whatever it takes, find him!" I pointed to two people and told them, "I want you to go back to the restaurant. If he's lost, he might go to the last place we were all together." As they ran out the door, I yelled, "Come back in thirty minutes and we'll regroup!"

In seconds, they were all on a mission. I stood alone in the lobby, and Becca was at the front desk asking them to send Logan's picture to the police. Moments later, Logan walked in with one of the leaders of the group that had split off. They must have just missed all the people running down the street looking for him. I yelled, "You're here and you're okay!" He must have thought I'd lost my mind. He didn't have a clue that we all thought he was lost in one of the biggest cities on earth.

Little Logan looked perplexed and stammered, "We didn't know you'd miss us. We just wanted to go a little farther to help more homeless people."

I wanted to tell him, "Don't ever feed homeless people again!" but I didn't. Becca came running in. Both of us hugged Logan, and I whispered, "Son, we love you so much!"

The better the plans, the more empowered your people will be. But even the best plans don't insulate you from problems.

This problem was all on me. I'm the Dad, and I would move heaven and earth to bring my boy back. I didn't expect others to feel as passionate as me, but they were magnificent in jumping in to look for Logan. And I didn't just sit and pray. Oh, there was prayer . . . really intense and really fast prayer . . . but no hesitation in taking action.

You'll prevent a lot of problems—and the biggest problems— by planning well. The better the plans, the more empowered your people will be. But even the best plans don't insulate you from problems. In every company, nonprofit organization, and church, leaders should expect the unexpected. Pop-up problems happen. It's a given. Plan how you'll respond by writing down the three questions, and then practice them again and again. Recognize your bent to catastrophize, isolate, or act impulsively, and counteract those tendencies by choosing to pull the card with the questions out of your back pocket and use them. You'll gain more confidence, you'll solve more problems, and your people will follow you anywhere.

Think about it:

1. Where do you fall on a continuum of careful planning on one end and fly-by-the-seat-of-your-pants intuition on the other?

....

Careful planning   **Intuitive**

2. What are the benefits and liabilities of your style? What needs to change?

3. What are some crises, minor and major, you've faced during the past year? How did you respond to each one?

4. How would it help you to stop and ask the three questions when you learn about a problem?

5. Who do you know who is cool and wise in a crisis? What can you learn from that person?

CHAPTER 3

ON TIME

Every decision has a runway. The takeoff may be as short as immediately, or it may extend to an hour, a day, a week, or several months. Leaders need to understand that the length of the runway for each decision is important. The time they take to decide can make or break the outcome.

When it's the leader's problem to fix, but he or she procrastinates, people notice. If it becomes a pattern, people lose faith. Soon they begin talking and asking pointed questions—not to the leader, but to each other. They wonder, "Doesn't he see what's going on?" "Why doesn't she do something about it?" Curiosity quickly turns to skepticism which can then morph into cynicism, and that's a big hole for a leader to climb out of.

Other leaders have the opposite problem. They make impulsive decisions rather than taking time to think through a complex issue that requires research and deliberation. Those leaders are the only ones who think it was smart to jump so fast. The people watching them have the same response as they do to those who take too long: they lose respect for their leaders.

One of the hardest decisions for most pastors is letting a staff member go. The church isn't a business. We're the body of Christ and the family of God. We report to the King of kings and the Shepherd of our souls, not shareholders or investors.

Most people who become pastors are tenderhearted and compassionate people. It's our joy to see people grow in their faith and thrive in their roles. We invest our time in them, but even more, we invest our hearts. Yet sometimes no matter how much training we provide and how much grace we give, things just don't work out. The idea of firing people questions their calling, at least to that place at that time, and it undercuts their livelihood and affects the welfare of their families. In addition, every staff member, even the least competent, is dearly loved by some people in the church. The decision almost inevitably creates shock waves throughout the congregation. When I talk to pastors about their roles, they tell me that firing a staff member, often who has become a friend, is perhaps the most gut-wrenching decision they have to make. It's no wonder many pastors drag their feet and give the person one more chance, and one more, and one more, and . . .

Actually, the church is a blend of a family and a business, with aspects of both. Yes, we all belong to our Heavenly Father, so we're family, but God has called us to participate in His purpose of seeking and saving the lost and making disciples of all nations. In that sense, all of us are employed in the family business.

Years ago, we had a man on our pastoral team who was highly competent in many aspects of church life. Steve had a keen mind and generated a lot of great ideas, not only for his areas of responsibility, but for many other ministries in our church. He had a unique blend of intelligence, perception about the culture, and organizational skills. Steve was one of the most productive staff members we've ever had. Many church members and staff appreciated his gifts, insights, energy, and effectiveness. With all those strengths, what could possibly go wrong?

The problem was that Steve walked into every meeting, and in fact, every conversation, with a hard edge of cynicism. He used his intelligence and insights to find fault in every person and every situation, and he very often ripped them to shreds. In addition, he made some very odd but definitive statements, such as, "When I have a kid, I'm never going to change a diaper."

When someone on our staff heard Steve make that ridiculously dramatic statement, she laughed and told him, "You can't be serious."

He almost snarled back, "I'm completely serious. Even if my kid has been sitting in poop for hours, I'll never change a diaper!" When he saw the incredulity on the face of everyone who overheard him, he went even further: "If my wife wants a kid, it's going to be her kid. She has to feed it, change it, get up with it at night, and do anything else the kid needs. I'm not a part of it."

Somebody else who was nearby shook his head and told Steve, "Oh, come on."

He barked back, "Not going to do it. You can count on that!"

But that wasn't an isolated instance of his harshness. One day in a staff meeting, we talked about how we could help a young lady whose mother had been abusive. Steve piped up, "I'm glad there's a hell for her mother. She's a loser."

Again, someone on the team pushed back, "Steve . . . you're not glad there's a hell for her."

"Yes, I am," he insisted. "She deserves it!"

People on the team looked at each other and rolled their eyes as if to say, "Can you believe that?" (We don't ever condone abuse in any form, but we always pray that everyone will repent and find grace and forgiveness for anything they've done.)

Steve was intensely loyal to his National Football League team. He wore jerseys and followed the stats of his favorite players. One day between services, I walked into the lobby and found him in a fierce argument with a guy who was wearing the jersey of another team. I walked over, grabbed him by the arm, pulled him away, and told him, "Stop it! You can't do that! You can't fight with people just because they like a different team! Jesus is more important than the Minnesota Vikings!" I took a deep breath and launched in again. "You were yelling at a guy who came to church to worship God! About loyalty to a football team! Do you have any idea how wrong that is?"

If I thought I'd made my point, I was badly mistaken. Steve transferred his anger to me. He snarled and yelled, "If I want to argue with someone about my team, that's my business, not yours!" (And then he said some things I won't repeat.)

I told him, "You are suspended for three days without pay. Leave the building right now. We'll talk again in three days, but unless you come back repentant, you're fired."

He came back three days later and we talked. He was grudgingly, barely on the edge of repentance. I should have seen that he wasn't ready to come back—that he was currently in no spiritual shape to be in the ministry—but we had a longstanding relationship and I wanted him to be repentant. I wanted to believe his change of heart was real. I wanted to avoid all the questions and the chaos that firing him would produce. I wanted to act like everything was just fine. Psychologists have a range of words to describe my choice to be blind to the truth, including *denial*, *minimizing, excusing,* and *rationalizing*—I was neck deep in all of them!

I was soon to discover exactly how bad the situation with Steve really was and how blind I was to the whole travesty. I had never taken a break from my church responsibilities, so I had scheduled a month-long sabbatical. I put Steve in charge of the church in my absence, and we also brought on a new assistant pastor, Joe, during that time.

While I was gone, Steve started telling people on our staff team, "You know, Pastor Rob ought to make me co-pastor. We do the same job. The only difference between him and me is that he signed the loan on the building." Then he barked, "If he doesn't make me co-pastor, I'm going to split this church and inflict maximum damage!" Even during the first staff meeting with Joe present, Steve repeatedly yelled profanity and then shouted, "If Pastor Rob doesn't make me co-pastor, I'm going to destroy this church!" (Instead of a gift basket for the new guy, we gave him this!)

Of course, I knew nothing about all this, but when I got back I sensed something was very wrong. It felt like a dark cloud had enveloped our staff team and our church. One day I ran into Joe, and I asked, "What's it like working at River Valley?"

He looked like I'd asked him if he was really an alien in a human body. After a long pause, he said, "Do you really want to know?"

"Sure. Tell me."

I thought he was going to say, "This is my dream job." He didn't. He said, "Pastor Rob, I feel defiled."

I was stunned. I mumbled, "What do you mean?"

Joe didn't miss a beat. "When you're not around, Steve uses horrible profanity. He obviously resents you, and he says he is committed to destroying this church if you don't make him co-pastor."

At that moment, the scales came off my eyes. I thought, *I knew it! I knew something was really wrong with Steve!* But until then I hadn't been able to put my finger on it. The others on the team were wondering why it was taking me so long to do something about an obvious problem. They were right. I was way too slow to fire him, but now I realized they had been complicit.

The next night, I had a meeting with the staff without Steve being present. I told them what Joe had shared with me. They concurred with Joe's report. They said Steve had been using extreme profanity for months when I wasn't around, and he had threatened often and clearly to destroy the church. They all said, "Pastor Rob, we're really sorry we didn't tell you about what was going on."

I agreed with them. If they didn't realize how angry and disappointed I felt, they soon found out when I told them, "You should be sorry. You disgust me. You know I never swear. How could you let someone curse so often behind my back and not tell me? And he told you he was going to destroy the church and inflict maximum damage if I didn't make him co-pastor. How could you listen to that betrayal and not let me know?"

I let that sink in for a few seconds, and then I told them, "You're all fired. If you want to keep your job, by 8:30 tomorrow morning you and your spouse need to write a letter of apology confessing to what you've done wrong and asking me to give you the grace of a chance to prove yourself. If you come repentant tomorrow morning, I'll put you on six months' probation. During that time, I can fire you for any cause. If you're done with me and River Valley, don't show up tomorrow. Your betrayal disgusts me. Now get out of here."

I then called the elders and discussed how we were going to fire Steve. I asked him to come to my house the next afternoon so we could work on something together. The elders parked around the corner so he wouldn't know they were waiting for him. When he walked through the door and saw them, he said, "We're not brainstorming about sermon ideas, are we?"

"No, we're not," I said matter-of-factly. "We're here to tell you that you're fired."

He was defiant. "Over what?"

"Profanity, threatening to split the church, and other destructive behaviors I could list, but the first two are enough. Steve, you need to repent. You need to find forgiveness in Jesus."

I hoped that would be the end of it, but I wasn't surprised when he wanted to argue. He glared at the elders and me: "There's nothing wrong with profanity. Words are just words."

At that point, he was pacing like a caged tiger. I said, "Sit down."

He growled, "I'll stand up if I want to!"

One of the businessmen on our elder board had had enough. He told Steve, "We haven't paid you to talk like a dock worker at my factory! We've paid you to be holy! There's everything wrong with profanity and your disloyal behavior. Now sit down and shut up!"

I told Steve, "I don't want you to come back to the church. We'll have someone box up your office and bring it to your house. You're done. Get help."

I hoped it was over. It wasn't. When the news got out, the people in our church were divided into three camps: some people thought Steve hung the moon and concluded that I had made a serious mistake; some were confused, but trusted me; and the elders and the people on our staff team were relieved that I had finally done what I should have done much sooner. I was terrified that Steve would, in fact, split the church and inflict incredible damage on all God had done at River Valley. I was afraid people would leave with him, and if they stayed, they'd harbor doubts about my ability to lead.

I didn't know how much the average congregation members knew or had seen. After all, I had only seen the problem clearly for a few hours, and it stunned me. If others had seen even part of all this for a while, they had every reason to wonder if I was up to the job. In fact, I was the blind man. Almost everybody else on staff was well aware of Steve's swearing, his threats, his violent temper, and his caustic effect on people.

Why was I so clueless? For the entire span of my friendship with Steve, he had been a glass half empty guy, and my perspective was always that the glass is half full. He had been brusque, harsh, and critical, but I thought, *Oh, that's just Steve. We can put up with him because he's so gifted and contributes so much to our church.* I didn't see the damage he was doing, but a lot of other people did. Later, when all of this came out, many of them told me they assumed I saw it all, but had some reason for overlooking it because Steve was my friend. Who were they, they asked, to step in and question someone I had known for so long?

By the way, all of our staff members and their spouses came to my office on time to give me their letters and ask for a second chance. They thanked me for the opportunity. I expected that, but I didn't expect the phone calls I received from the parents of some of them who thanked me for being gracious to their children. One of them said, "From the bottom of my heart, I want to thank you for giving my family another chance."

The decision to fire Steve was mine alone. I did it, I owned it, but I spent way too much time on the runway before making the call. The delay caused people to doubt me. For a long time (without knowing how bad the situation really was), I had rationalized keeping him on, and I defended the decision in my mind many times—but I was wrong to wait.

This was a pivotal moment in my leadership. It's the biggest problem I've had to fix as a pastor. It was a risky move to fire Steve, but I would have risked much more if I hadn't. I was terrified that my ignorance and blindness had caused irreparable harm, and I was angry—appropriately angry—with my staff team for leaving me in the dark. In that moment, it felt like everything was on the line. I had to tell myself, *I'm going to do the right thing no matter what it costs.* I realized it could easily become a lose-lose proposition: if I fired him, the church could split, and if I didn't, I'd lose the respect of those who saw me as weak.

After Steve and the elders left my house that afternoon, my adrenaline level crashed, and I felt utterly depleted. Normally I would take a nap, but I just wanted to cry. How could I have missed this so badly? What kind of leader was I? Was I missing anything else?

And finally, I had to tell the congregation. The next Sunday morning I told them we were having a special meeting that night because I had some important news to share with them. As a practice, I don't share bad news in worship services where there are visitors, and I was pretty sure the visitors wouldn't attend a special church meeting at night. That night, I explained that I had let Steve go. I didn't go into many details, but I made sure everyone knew the elders and I had gone through a careful process and were unanimous in the decision. As people filed out, a man came up to me and said, "Pastor Rob, I didn't think you saw it."

After all that had happened in the previous days, I had a good idea what he was talking about, but I asked, "What do you mean?"

He smiled as he said, "I wasn't sure you saw what the rest of us had seen in Steve and his destructive and negative attitude. I thought that if you saw it but you didn't do anything about it, you don't have the courage to lead our church."

I was shocked and embarrassed. While I was recovering from his statement, another businessman walked up and interrupted: "Good job, Pastor Rob. You finally pulled the trigger. I was going to call and offer you $100 to fire Steve, but I'll keep my money now."

What? A guy in the church was planning to pay me to fire somebody? He not only knew the problem was real, but he had thought of a way to prod me to do my job—the job only I could do. That night my shock and embarrassment multiplied. I had been so foolish, so blind, so slow to do what obviously needed to be done.

(Obviously, this story about Steve is painful to tell—and probably painful to read—but I want to be honest about the strain this put on me and my team. I've always been wide open to reconciliation, and I regularly pray for him. Someday, I hope Steve will call and we'll start the process of rebuilding our relationship. I'm sure God would be thrilled with that.)

The Right Time

This painful experience with Steve showed me that I had to determine the right time for the decisions I make as a leader. Each situation is different, but each one has a runway of a specific length. As the pilot, if I wait too long to take off, I'll crash at the end of the runway. I was certainly left in a crumpled heap in my relationship with Steve. I couldn't let that happen again over any decision that had to be made.

Each situation is different, but each one has a runway of a specific length. As the pilot, if I wait too long to take off, I'll crash at the end of the runway.

For instance, if a church is at eighty percent capacity in worship (where the experts say people start to feel crowded and uncomfortable), the pastor may consider a second service. The question is: when is the right time to launch it? Easter is packed out, but the summer is coming. The church may feel pretty full during May, but there will be lower attendance during the summer. It's best to launch the new service in early September when school starts, excitement is in the air, and churches traditionally have an influx of visitors.

Or suppose a volunteer has been faithfully leading a ministry, but it has become apparent the demands of the role have gone beyond the person's capacity, either in the level of skill required or the time needed to organize and oversee it. Is the problem severe enough that the ministry is really suffering and a change needs to be made right away, or is there time for a more graceful transition to a new leader?

In staff positions, we become aware that we need to hire additional people or perhaps fire, promote, or move someone laterally to a position that's a better fit. Again, the question of timing makes a difference. If you move too slowly, you risk your credibility and blunt any momentum. But if you move too fast, you might bruise people's feelings, which could be minimized if you wait for a season in the church calendar when people expect changes to occur, like the beginning of the school year or the first of the calendar year.

Leaders also need to be shrewd about timing when renting, buying and refurbishing, or building new facilities. Some pastors anticipate growth and move their churches to bigger facilities, but they don't notice the shift in community demographics, and the surge doesn't happen. They are left facing a large mortgage or rent payment every month as they encourage people in a mostly empty worship space to give generously. That's stress! Yet other pastors are too timid to trust God with their church's growth. They pack people in for so long that many find other churches that are either permanent or not as crowded.

Although timing is essential, we don't need to look for a specific minute on a particular day to make the call. Most decisions have a reasonable window in which to respond, and acting at any time within the window works well. A large part of the equation is how we communicate the decision. If we don't provide adequate information soon enough, people fill in the blanks with their own version of reality, and the gossip mill runs on overdrive. Or if we don't explain personnel decisions clearly enough, we can appear heartless to the people outside the immediate circle of those who know the whole story.

When Moses gave instructions to the people of Israel to prepare them for their trip across the desert to the Promised Land, he said, "Our livestock too must go with us; not a hoof is to be left behind" (Exodus 10:26). They had taken spoil from the

Egyptians as they left, including herds of cattle. Moses was explaining that the mass of people who were fleeing slavery to find rest and safety in the land God was giving them could only travel as fast as the slowest cow. In the same way, leaders need to be sure we take everybody with us on the journey. We may want to move at Mach 5, but many of our people can only advance at a slow and steady pace.

Although timing is essential, we don't need to look for a specific minute on a particular day to make the call. Most decisions have a reasonable window in which to respond, and acting at any time within the window works well.

From countless conversations with pastors over the years, I'm confident that far more of them make decisions too slowly than too quickly. Something always keeps them from pulling the trigger: they want more information, they need one more staff member, they want the thumbs up from one more elder or key donor, or something else. Each delay makes perfect sense at the time, but if they stand back and look at the pattern, it's clear they're avoiding the risk of trusting God for something bigger and better than before.

As the choices of avoiding the decision add up, inertia has its own momentum. Gradually, it gets harder and harder to say, "Let's do this!" The pastor and the church stay stuck. The mood of the rest of the leaders in the church is like a rubber raft with a pinhole leak. Slowly, imperceptibly, the air goes out, the raft gets squishy, and it's harder to move it even a small distance. Any momentum is history, and visionary, skilled, assertive people go somewhere else.

When it comes to people decisions, churches are very different from businesses. If a corporation fires an assistant accountant on the fifth floor, customers don't call in to express their outrage. But when a pastor fires someone in any visible position, a lot of people are at least concerned, probably confused, and perhaps more than a little angry that their favorite staff member was treated unfairly . . . or so they assume. He has fired someone's best friend, the youth leader who means so much to their child, or a beloved source of comfort who came to the hospital to pray for a relative. Some situations, like the one with Steve, require immediate action. For those, we need to communicate as clearly and as soon as possible, first to other leaders and then to the church family. But in cases when the problem isn't a moral failure or unrepentant defiance, we have more time to prepare the person and those involved.

When I think of decisions that are on me to make as I lead, I think of traveling with my kids on a road trip when they were young. If one of them said, "Dad, I need to go to the bathroom," I asked, "I need to know: Do I need to pull the car over on the side of the road because you're about to make a mess in your pants? Do I need to find the first gas station at the next exit? Or can you hold it for thirty minutes until we get to our scheduled stop?" If I don't know the answer to those questions, our family trip, and the aroma of our car for the next month, may be up for grabs!

This is a very practical grid to help me understand the timing of decisions. For instance, one of our elders came to me and said, "Pastor Rob, the volunteer in charge of the ushers isn't doing a good job, and I don't think he's up to it. I think you need to make a change."

I responded, "I see what you see, and yes, I'm on it. I'm going to make a change, but not right now. I think it's best to wait for three things: the right person to replace him, the right responsibility for the one we're moving out, and the right time to make the move." I continued, "This isn't a business. You can make a personnel change in an instant, but that's not how we do it." Then I explained my thinking in more detail. The elder was satisfied that I fully understood the situation and had a plan for a seamless transition.

Your Time

If you assume you always make decisions in the perfect window of timing, you're probably smoking something. All of us are in process, and we probably need at least a tweak if not a major overhaul of our grasp of timing. A few of us need to slow down, but most of us need to dig deep to find the courage to move when we need to. If you try to avoid tough decisions, you'll fail to be a good leader. Almost all the hard choices we make involve risk and pain. We'll hurt some feelings, and we'll get some pushback. That's unavoidable for leaders. Those difficult dilemmas comprise the five percent of decisions that are entirely ours, and they make or break our ability to have a profoundly positive impact on people.

If you try to avoid tough decisions, you'll fail to be a good leader. Almost all the hard choices we make involve risk and pain.

One of the reasons we feel so much weight of the burden is that we think it's up to us to make everybody on our team, on our board, and in the congregation happy with us. Subconsciously, we think we're their source of wisdom, love, and strength. I was disabused of this idea one day as I read the biblical account of Abraham sending Hagar away (Genesis 16). In that moment, Hagar was homeless and destitute, despised by Sarah and reject-ed by Abraham. An angel of the Lord appeared to her and said, "I will increase your descendants so much that they will be too nu-merous to count." The angel promised she would have a son, and Hagar responded in a prayer to God, "You are the God who sees me! I have now seen the One who sees me" (Genesis 16:9, 13).

Through this passage, God showed me that I'm not the source for the people in my church, even those who work most closely with me. God is their source, and God is their very great reward (Genesis 15:1). Am I as jealous and cruel as Sarah? I sure hope not. Am I as seemingly heartless as Abraham? I don't think so. Still, I can't be the fountain of life for the people entrusted to me. I can trust that God will supply me with wisdom and strength to lead, and He'll supply others with wisdom and strength to fol-low and serve. This biblical insight has rolled a huge burden from my shoulders to God's. This freedom has helped me make better decisions about timing because anxiety doesn't cause me to be impulsive, and fear doesn't paralyze me.

We want to wrap every decision about people with a spirit of love and generosity. We give a long runway when people want to make a move, and we give a generous severance package when a person's gifts and capacity can't keep up with the growth of the church. The vast majority of the people who leave us are wonder-ful people who truly love God and serve Him with all their hearts.

It's easy to be gracious to them, and it's much harder to see them go than someone who is demanding, defiant, and threatens the life of the church.

Most of us are well aware that we own the problems, and it's up to us to fix them. It's time for us to look at how our fear of failure and criticism affects our decision-making, causing us to be impulsive or avoidant. We can learn to find the window for major decisions, and we can learn to communicate with clarity and grace to the people affected by them.

Right There with You

I don't want people to think I'm talking down to anyone when I give advice about leadership. If I've learned anything, I've learned it the hard way. I think I'm known as a visionary, make-it-happen leader, but two of my biggest blunders happened because I didn't make the necessary move. I've told the story about Steve; the other one is about the idea of starting a second service in the first years of the church. I was so afraid of making a mistake, I couldn't bring myself to make the jump. And I wasn't too quick to realize my error. We didn't add a second service for three years, and during that time, our attendance chart looked like a highway in Kansas . . . flat!

The window of opportunity may close quickly. In any organization, the use of technology can propel it forward, but only if the leaders anticipate the benefits and have the courage to take a risk on the future. In a humorous (if sometimes painful) *Forbes* article, "It Seemed Like a Good Idea at the Time: 7 of the Worst Business Decisions Ever Made," Erika Anderson takes us back to the dawn of another era of innovation in communication:

In 1876, William Orten was President of Western Union, which had a monopoly on the most advanced communications technology available, the telegraph. Orten was offered the patent on a new invention, the telephone, for $100,000 (worth about $2M in current dollars). He considered the whole idea ridiculous, and wrote directly to Alexander Graham Bell, saying, "After careful consideration of your invention, while it is a very interesting novelty, we have come to the conclusion that it has no commercial possibilities...What use could this company make of an electrical toy?" Two years later, after the telephone began to take off, Orten realized the magnitude of his mistake, and spent years (unsuccessfully) challenging Bell's patents.[3]

Sometimes people in our church come up with innovative ideas—and some of them are really bad! One man came up to me after a fundraising appeal and suggested the church take out up to a $100,000 insurance policy on every person in the congregation. As long as we paid the low premium, we could collect even if the people who died had left our church. He explained that Wal-Mart used this practice and cashed in on employees who died. (The *New York Times* reported a lawsuit against the company for this practice.[4]) For an instant, I thought, *That's a great idea!* But then I realized the conflicts of interest I would face when I visited people in the hospital. If they got well, I could praise God. If they died, we got the money. If the church needed some cash, how would I pray at that moment? Man, I couldn't live with that! (But for the record, I *always* pray for healing and recovery!)

Another man came to see me. He said, "Pastor, if you'll give me $100,000 of the church's money, I'll go to the casino and double it." I must have looked like I didn't believe him because he immediately told me, "I guarantee it."

I was certain I wasn't giving him the money, but I was curious. I asked, "What's your system? Why are you so confident you can win?"

He grinned, "The slots."

There was no window of optimum time for me to give $100,000 of the church's money to this guy! I have tremendous respect for people who take the initiative to come up with new ideas, but not all of them are good ones.

Know your tendencies in timing and make any necessary adjustments. Most of us need a shot of courage to take advantage of opportunities, but some of us need to slow down and be a bit more deliberate. Great decisions are only great if they're timely.

Think about it:

1. On a continuum of timing in making decisions, are you too fast or too slow? Mark where you think you are on the scale.

....

Too fast   **Just right**   **Too slow**

2. Where would your spouse put you on the scale? How about the people who work closely with you?

3. What are some benefits and consequences of your natural pace?

4. What needs to change in your timing of decisions, and how would the change help you be a better leader?

5. How would you describe the window of timing for important decisions? How can you tell when it begins and ends for:

   • a personnel change?

   • moving or building?

   • starting another service?

6. How does seeing God as the source, for you and everyone else involved, free you from anxiety and fear so you can make timely decisions?

PART 2

IT'S UP TO *THEM*

CHAPTER 4

I KNOW A GUY . . .

Because our church has grown and now has resources, pastors of young churches sometimes call me to ask for money. Some have not have raised enough to launch their church. Others have encountered unexpected expenses. Whatever the cause, they're in trouble. When they call or meet with me at a conference, I listen carefully, but I almost always tell them, "I could help you, but it wouldn't be the best thing for you. There's something about the struggle that makes us stronger, and I don't want to get in the way of God's using this situation to teach you important lessons about depending on Him."

Does that sound heartless? I haven't come to this perspective easily. As I've described, for many years I tried like crazy to be "the guy," the person everyone could count on, the hero of every situation, the fixer of every problem. It almost killed me. I learned very slowly, but I eventually got it: I'm definitely responsible for fixing certain problems, but not all of them. Quite often, I need to shove the weight of responsibility to the people on my team—my elders, my leaders, and the people in my congregation . . . and to pastors who ask me for financial help.

When God was teaching me this point of view, I heard an illustration about chicks hatching from their eggs: the struggle to break out is necessary for them to get stronger and survive. I could have checked this story out on Snopes or the Ag department of a major university, but instead, I found a better source: myPetChicken.com. Here's the straight scoop:

> Generally speaking you will NOT want to intervene in the hatching process when incubating fertile eggs. [If the chick is in real trouble] you *may* decide to help, but be forewarned! It is VERY easy to cause the chick to bleed to death when you try helping him out of the shell. You don't want to watch that happen and feel that responsibility. Further, opening the incubator to assist this one chick lets even more humidity out of your incubator, and makes it more likely that OTHER chicks will have problems escaping the shell. This just isn't a decision to make lightly. It's easy to cause more problems than you had to begin with.[5]

Did you get all that? Even when the chick is in real trouble, the farmer (or new chicken parent) can cause fatal damage to the little bird if he tries to help, and helping one can cause significant problems for the other chicks. The struggle produces strength—for the individual chick and for the rest of the clutch—that can't happen any other way. The last line is one leaders need to burn into our memories: "It's easy to cause more problems than you had to begin with." Thank you for that brilliant leadership principle, myPetChicken.com!

A Higher Principle

Human nature, especially compassionate human nature, says that if we possess the power to help someone, we have to. But the best leaders know that's not always true. In fact, a higher principle exists. When I take responsibility that should be given to others, nothing good happens. I get exhausted and become resentful, and the people around me don't have the opportunity to develop their faith muscles, their fundraising muscles, their creativity muscles, their prayer muscles, and their tenacity muscles. In other words, when I thought I was helping them, I was actually hurting them.

When I take responsibility that should be given to others, nothing good happens.

Leadership expert Ken Blanchard observes that too often, managers (and pastors) let others "put a monkey on our backs"—and many foolishly take monkeys from others when one monkey is enough of a load for anyone. In "The Art of Managing Monkeys," he explains,

> Managers must be careful not to pick up other people's monkeys. When they do, they broadcast the message that the employees lack the skills to care for and feed the monkeys themselves. Managers who grab monkeys off their people's backs often kill employee initiative, and everyone is left waiting for the boss to "make the next move."
>
> Nobody wins when you take care of other people's monkeys. You become a hassled manager and don't feel very good about yourself. And you have workers who look to satisfy their needs elsewhere, because they feel underutilized and unappreciated. They often become dependent upon the boss. The care and feeding of other people's monkeys is the ultimate lose/lose deal.[6]

In the early years of River Valley when we were a portable church, I didn't manage monkeys very well at all. In fact, all the monkeys were on my back. As I've described, I picked up the truck on Saturday, loaded it early on Sunday morning, set up, changed clothes, preached, packed up, stored everything, and took the truck back. But that's not all. I sent handwritten birthday and anniversary cards to every person and couple in the church. When it was just a dozen of us, it wasn't a big task, but as we grew, so did the stack of cards going out. Whenever one of our people suffered any kind of crisis, I was counselor, pastor, chaplain, organizer, caterer, moving guy, and any other role they needed me to play.

I was fairly proficient at some of those roles, but when the truck broke down, I was clueless. I remember going to the auto parts store, buying Thrust starting fluid and spraying it in the carburetor as flames leaped from the engine! Things like this sometimes happened on Sunday morning, so after I got the truck running (no small miracle there), unloaded, and set up, I smelled like I'd worked all week at a local garage. To be honest, when I met people in the hospital or the funeral home to comfort them, I tried my best, but I'm a lousy counselor. Some people know just the right things to say—I'm not one of them. But it didn't dawn on me that I could refer grieving and struggling people to a competent professional. I assumed I had to be the hero in every circumstance.

I understand the drive to be everything to everyone. At a pastor's retreat, the leader asked the pastors to call out the tasks they were responsible to fulfill. They stopped at thirty-five, including outstanding preaching, discipling board members, consistent personal evangelism, being an exemplary spouse and parent and a leader in the community, raising money, and setting an example of hours of personal devotions each week. The leader then asked, "How many of those do you need to do yourself and do with excellence?" The group erupted in a combination of laughter and groans. In unison, many voices shouted, "All of them!" As they talked, many of the pastors realized they had very unrealistic expectations of themselves—and they had cultivated unrealistic expectations among their people by presenting themselves as the hero of every situation. They had been absolutely sure it was up to them to keep all the plates spinning, continually add more plates, make everybody happy, right every wrong, see an awakening among the lost and revival among the saved. But they felt tired, used up, and unappreciated. And while the pastors were doing so much, their people hadn't been encouraged, or even allowed, to use their gifts in service to others. The pastors were burned out (or getting there fast), and they had trained their people to be passive.

I wanted people to see me as the one they could count on when no one else cared. I needed to feel needed, and I thrived on the encouragement I received when I fixed people's problems. There's probably nothing wrong with that perspective if you're a chaplain, but if you're a leader, it's deadly. Don't misunderstand: compassion is a great quality to have. In fact, it's the word that describes Jesus' emotions more than all others combined. But Jesus trained people, delegated to them, gave them authority, and released them to change the world. That's our role as leaders too.

A turning point came when I recognized the painful fact that I was seeking the approval of people more than the approval of God. For me, and I suspect for many others, repentance is a vital part of the process of change so that I want God's will for people, including letting them struggle, more than my will to be "the guy." When I understood the limits of my role and responsibility,

I began helping people develop their faith muscles instead of their phone call muscles asking me for help. A church grows only to the extent of the pastor's ability to delegate well. I hadn't delegated because I wanted all the attention and all the credit, but I started learning a new way to live.

When I talk to pastors, I sometimes use the illustration that some of us are "sugar pastors," some are "fruits and vegetables pastors," and some are "protein pastors." Sugar pastors give people a high on Sunday morning, but they (and the people who drink their sugar) have nothing left for the rest of the week. It's all a show, and they thrive on their Sunday morning reputations. This can be true of others too: youth pastors, music leaders, and teachers. Fruits and vegetables pastors are faithful and dedicated to their teams, but they don't provide enough nourishment to give their people the strength they need to excel. Protein pastors infuse a source of power into the staff, board members, and volunteers so they can take responsibility, serve with authority, reach far beyond the walls of the church, and build more leaders wherever they go. Even if they aren't the biggest stars on Sunday, they're equipping the body to function with power, purpose, and persistence.

Many small churches hire a sugar pastor because they want people to experience a high on Sunday morning. It's their only marketing tool. The pastor then hires friends who are fruits and vegetables staff and can organize their teams fairly well, but until the pastor learns to provide protein, the church won't fulfill God's calling. The ministry of the church isn't about one person who shines on Sunday morning while everyone else observes. It's about building up people so they play their God-given roles with joy, enthusiasm, and effectiveness.

When a pastor delivers protein to the staff and volunteers, those people become "the guys" and "the gals" who enthusiastically step up to get the job done. And then they provide protein to their teams, and those people step up. When this happens, the culture of the church radically changes. Every leader is building leaders, and more people want God to use them to make a difference. More people say, "I'll do it. I'll make it happen. I'll trust God. You can count on me."

Let me be painfully honest. I was so much the sugar pastor that I had to be fully in charge our church picnic one Sunday afternoon. You would have seen me that morning before church running through the grocery store buying everything we needed, pushing two carts full of brats and buns and everything else, frantic when I couldn't find the mayonnaise, and sweating to get it all done in time for me to rush to the stage and look like the man of the hour to the people in the seats ready for the sermon.

I know the transition from sugar to protein pastor can happen because I did it. I was a sugar pastor and I hired sugar staff. It was a colossal mess. I tried to do everything, and my true motives were revealed when I resented other people getting more credit than I got. When our church grew to about 500, I reached the absolute limits of my capacity. I was angry that I was doing so much and felt so little appreciation. I hated being a sugar pastor, but I was addicted to the lifestyle. (I could have been described as a "diabetic pastor.") Something—but I had no idea what—had to change. I wondered, *What is going to happen now? I can't do ministry like this much longer.*

As I thought and prayed, I came up with two options: We could plant more churches in the city that never got above my limit of 500, or I could change my ministry philosophy, strategy, and leadership style to equip leaders at River Valley to take more responsibility. I didn't have the culinary leadership terms yet, but I made a commitment to stop being a sugar pastor and start being a protein pastor. My perspective had to change. I had assumed being a pastor was always and only "hands on," but I realized it's far more "hands open." It's not *me* but *we*, encouraging people to identify their gifts and passions and step into responsibilities where they could flourish.

I had assumed being a pastor was always and only "hands on," but I realized it's far more "hands open." It's not *me* but *we*.

The change didn't happen quickly or smoothly. For about a year, I struggled and grieved. I had felt so strongly that I had to be the hero that it was incredibly difficult to make any progress. I realize now that my whole identity was caught up in being Super Pastor. There were times during that year when I found out someone was in the hospital. Our new plan was to assign other pastors to do hospital visits, and we contacted the person's Life Group leader to care for the person and the family, but I felt so guilty and so compulsive about my need to show up that I went anyway. When I walked into the room, I'd see the pastor and people from the group doing exactly what we had equipped and released them to do, and I felt so conflicted. I was happy others were doing what I'd been doing so long, but I felt sad they didn't really need me. I knew it was right, but it felt so wrong.

Gradually, what felt wrong became only awkward and finally began to feel right. I became more comfortable sharing the load with others, not just for hospital visits but in every aspect of the church's life. I went to the hospital less often. After a while, I joked that if I showed up, they had better have their will written and signed! After I said that one Sunday morning, a dear lady in our church was in the hospital, and I went to visit her. When she saw me walk in, she said, "It must be worse than I thought. I guess I'm dying!" I assured her that her doctor hadn't called me with any bad news. I just wanted her to know that I loved her and cared for her and had asked to do her visit. She looked relieved.

As I shared responsibility, authority, and opportunities with other people, I was careful to avoid isolating myself behind a wall of delegation. I'm not just a leader; I'm a pastor, and I still want to care for people in their time of need. I can't care for everybody, but I can care for some. I need to delegate well and empower people to minister, but for my heart's sake and as an example to others, I need to stay engaged in pastoring people in their darkest hours. Today I have limits on my time and availability, but there are no limits on my care for people. I'm not the CEO of a business; I am and will always be the pastor of a church.

Our church has grown and needs me to be a visionary and an administrative leader, but my primary role, God's calling in my life, is to be a pastor. I need to remember this fact, and my people need to know it. No matter how large our church gets and how much I delegate to others, I'll pastor our staff and our board, and I'll pastor others in the church when it's good and right. Even as I'm working on this chapter away from home, I'm changing my flight to go back early so I can officiate at a funeral for one of our deacons. I'm sure others on our pastoral staff would do a great job comforting the family and leading the service, but I want to be there.

And I still send handwritten birthday and anniversary cards to our staff, their spouses, and all of their children. I include a $30 gift card to Target in the cards to the pastors' kids, and I send a $100 card to the couples so they can enjoy dinner together. I can't do that for the thousands in our church, but I can communicate my heart to the circle closest to me, and they can pay it forward to the people whose lives they touch, and then to their circles, and on and on.

"I've Got This!"

As I've learned to give responsibility to others, I've seen some amazing things happen. Over and over again, I've identified a problem, and people have eagerly stepped up to fix it. They would never have done that if I'd continued to be responsible for everything, but thankfully, we've created a culture of shared values and shared responsibilities which produces shared effort and shared celebration. It's a glorious thing when I talk about a need to my staff or elders and someone says, "Pastor Rob, I know a guy who can fix this." In those moments, I know our leaders understand that none of us is expected to be the lone hero. One of our primary tasks as leaders is to identify and empower a host of heroes!

A storm came through the city and a tornado ripped part of the roof off the church. As I stood and looked at the water pouring into the building, I realized I wasn't going to have any time to prepare my sermon that week if I took care of the leak . . . but a man standing next to me put his hand on my shoulder and said, "Pastor, I've got this." I looked at him like he was an angel when he told me, "I'll contact the insurance company, and I'll put a patch on the roof until it can be permanently repaired."

I could have said, "Oh, no. You're way too busy to tackle this," but I didn't. I said, "Thank you so much. Call the office and get the insurance information. If you need anything else, let my office know."

If we keep our eyes open, we'll find capable and willing people who are eager to step up and step in to solve a problem. For instance . . .

- A church may have been planning and preparing for a mission trip for a year, but days before the group is scheduled to leave, the leader needs emergency surgery (or a child gets sick, or any of a hundred other crises). The pastor wonders if the trip will have to be canceled, but someone scheduled to go (or perhaps someone out of the blue) says, "Pastor, I've got this. I'll go. I've been on trips like this before, and I know what needs to happen. Get me the information, and I'll take care of everything."

- A growing church needs more parking space, but they don't have enough money budgeted to cover it. The pastor shares the need with the church board, and one of the men says, "I believe God's hand is on this church. I'll give half of the money, and I'll find others who are good for the rest."

- Quite often, the need we identify is outside the range of our expertise and experience. For me, if there's a mechanical problem, I'm in deep weeds. I assume every problem is caused by faulty bushings. (I have no idea what those are, but I heard a mechanic use the term one day.) When we were a portable church, everything depended on our truck. If the transmission went out or there was a problem with the engine, I was helpless and in a panic. I needed someone to come along and say, "Pastor Rob, I'll take care of it." He would either reach into his vehicle, pull out a box of tools, and make the repair on the spot (it always astounds me that people can do that), or he would call a mechanic, have it repaired, and get a replacement truck we could use until the repair was completed.

Could I have gotten the roof repaired, led the mission trip, raised money for a parking lot, or fixed the truck? "Yes" to the first three and a resounding "No!" to the last one. But if I had taken ownership of those solutions, I would have robbed other people of the joy of using their gifts and resources for the glory of God. I've come to the startling conclusion that God has put it in the hearts of His people to long to serve in a way that challenges them and gives them joy. My job isn't to be the hero, but to make heroes of as many people as possible. And as we all trust Jesus together, we realize He is the ultimate hero we can count on.

As my leadership model has shifted to give responsibility to others, I've seen many people rise to the occasion and do things they would never have gotten to do if I'd kept trying to do their jobs for them. People on our staff team are incredibly creative, and this model has unleashed their spirit of innovation. When they know they have both the responsibility and the authority, they're highly motivated to achieve their goals with excellence. Are there problems? Of course. Wherever there's more than one person, there will be tension, at least occasionally, but sharing responsibility almost always has multiplied benefits.

As my leadership model has shifted to give responsibility to others, I've seen many people rise to the occasion and do things they would never have gotten to do if I'd kept trying to do their jobs for them.

On youth league basketball teams, sometimes one kid takes all the shots. Even if he's a spectacular player, this isn't a winning strategy because the rest of the team becomes passive and demoralized. On really good teams, ball movement is a sign of great teamwork. Everybody touches the ball, and everybody takes open shots. I've noticed that in the NCAA tournament, commonly known as March Madness, players often come off the bench and make critical shots that make the difference in the game. They made them only because the coach put them in and someone passed them the ball. That's my role on our team: to put people in the game and make sure they get the ball. I've had instances when someone I would never have considered, like the custodian, came through to solve a problem that had nothing to do with his area of expertise or responsibility. It's a wonderful thing to see.

When we pass people the ball, we're giving them authority as well as responsibility. The two must go together or people will feel very confused, and soon they'll be angry. In an article for *Inc.*, Peter Economy advises:

> Anytime you delegate a task, you also need to delegate the authority—the organizational power and resources—required to get the job done. Without this, your employees [and volunteers] will have a much harder time doing what you've asked. They may even become frustrated and resentful that you've given them assignments that they cannot reasonably complete.[7]

No one likes being on a team and never getting the ball. When we put people in the game, we need to make sure they understand they have the authority to shoot. They'll miss from time to time, but that's okay. They'll never make shots if we don't empower them to shoot.

Size Doesn't Matter

The principle of the chicks (allowing struggle to promote personal growth) applies no matter how big your church is. In a small church, you can probably do it all, but don't! Even in a church plant when you have only a handful of people, share responsibility—for your sanity's sake and to build up the people around you. The kingdom of God isn't built by one overcommitted, unwise, exhausted sugar pastor. The kingdom is built only when we empower everyone who is willing to take ownership of a role and do all they do to the glory of God.

The Apostle Paul explained that our role isn't primarily to be doers, but to mobilize many doers. (If he had known about protein, he might have used that analogy!) He wrote: "So Christ himself gave the apostles, the prophets, the evangelists, the pastors and teachers, to equip his people for works of service, so that the body of Christ may be built up until we all reach unity in the faith and in the knowledge of the Son of God and become mature, attaining to the whole measure of the fullness of Christ" (Ephesians 4:11-13). Isn't that what we want for our people, to attain "to the whole measure of the fullness of Christ"? Super Pastors may receive a lot of accolades, but they don't fulfill this mandate from God.

Some would say, "Well, my people aren't strong in their faith. They need me to disciple them for a long time before they're ready." Maybe, maybe not. Wherever Paul traveled, he preached the gospel of grace, led people to Christ, appointed elders, and left them to lead their fledgling churches. They didn't have church growth resources, books on leadership, and conferences where they could learn new strategies. They had only Paul's commission, the Old Testament Scriptures, and the Holy Spirit. His letters and the Gospels were circulating to the cities, but their libraries could have fit in a mailbox. To be sure, some people, then and now, aren't ready for the roles of leadership, but Paul didn't appoint everybody as elders. He selected some, undoubtedly after much prayer and the leading of the Holy Spirit, and he found enough people in every city who took the ball and ran with it.

Branch Rickey was the general manager of the Brooklyn Dodgers who took the risk to bring Jackie Robinson to the Major Leagues in 1947. Rickey was a devout Christian with a brilliant baseball mind and a flair for dramatic statements. Some people criticized him for how he handled the team. They believed he should leave players in the minors longer so they would be better developed before they came to the major-league team. Rickey saw that those players were so excited about being there that he could live with the mistakes they made. He told his detractors: "I prefer errors of enthusiasm to the indifference of wisdom."[8] I do too.

If we have the courage to share the load and believe in people, it will be messy at times and they'll make mistakes, but most often, they will be errors of enthusiasm. I can live with that.

Every leadership model has strengths and liabilities. Far too often, pastors try to hold on too tightly to the reins of leadership. For a variety of reasons—fear, inexperience, ignorance, the desire for acclaim, and others—they insist on being the guy, the hero of every story. If we have the courage to share the load and believe in people, it will be messy at times and they'll make mistakes, but most often, they will be errors of enthusiasm. I can live with that.

When you start sharing responsibilities, you will discover that "the guy" may not be a guy. Women play key roles in all of our churches. And "the guy" may not be a paid staff member, a key volunteer, or a big donor. If we have believing hearts and open minds, we'll see that God brings a mechanic when the truck breaks down, an electrician when we blow a circuit, a quiet person who agrees to lead a group, a roofer when rain is pouring in, and a person who steps up to lead a mission trip when the leader gets sick. I believe those people are all around us, waiting for us to notice them and let them serve God with all their might.

As I've faced problems I couldn't fix, I looked for God to bring someone to help me. Sometimes they were people in the church. Others were people in the community whom I treated as valued friends, and many indeed became friends. They started attending our church, some came to faith in Christ, and a few have become leaders. Like everyone in the structure of our church as we develop our leadership pipeline, we want to equip them, inspire them, find where they are most excited to contribute, give them plenty of resources, and continually encourage them like crazy. Of course, some people need more help than others, but we always lean toward believing God is working to give them His heart, His vision, and His energy. By now, it's really not about me at all.

In this leadership model, I assure you there will be messes. It's guaranteed. But unexpected problems will be overwhelmed by the blessings God will pour out on your church as your people become passionate and active in advancing the kingdom. Each one is a chick who needs to struggle to grow stronger. We may be tempted to jump in to make things easier for them, but if we do, we're limiting them, hurting the church, and abdicating our role of equipping people to serve God with their whole hearts. Put your chicks in places where they can struggle and grow strong.

Think about it:

1. What applications can you make from the concept of letting the chick break out of its shell?

2. How would you describe the blend and balance of a pastor's heart of compassion and the need to let people struggle so they develop faith muscles?

3. Are you a sugar pastor, a fruits and vegetables pastor, or a protein pastor? Explain your answer.

4. What are some concrete steps you can take to become more of a protein pastor?

5. The transition from Super Pastor to a disciple developer often goes through a cycle starting with feeling wrong, then awkwardness, and finally feeling right. Where are you in this cycle? What is your advice for pastors in this transition who feel like it's wrong?

6. Can you live with the "errors of enthusiasm" in the people you lead? Why or why not?

7. What difference has it made (or will it make) for you and your people if you equip others to own aspects of your church's ministry?

CHAPTER 5

BITE-SIZED

When my son Connor graduated from North Central University in 2015, I asked him to become our Connections Pastor who is responsible for the entire process from the first day people drive into our parking lot until they join a small group and find a place to serve. It includes overseeing the parking lot attendants, the welcome center, the greeters and ushers, and the system to connect people to group leaders and ministry coordinators. Connor's responsibility was to give clear directions and heartfelt motivation to hundreds of people who serve in these areas.

Connor had been in his role for only a few weeks when he noticed that the old adage about churches applied to River Valley as well: our church was like a football game where a few people were on the field giving all they've got while thousands watched and cheered from the stands. In our case, he saw a few people in each ministry area who worked tirelessly while numerous others served only sporadically. The motives of the hardworking people were probably as mixed as mine had been: they saw a need and wanted God to use them to meet it (that's the noble side), but they tended to get a little too much identity out of being the people "everyone can count on" (drifting over to the compulsive side). Many are the sweetest, most good-natured people, yet if leaders overuse them, they can become prideful because they're doing more than anyone else, or they might resent the burden of all the expectations and burn out . . . or both.

Counting on overworked, overcommitted people may get the job done in the short run, but it almost inevitably has negative long-term effects on everyone involved.

How does this happen? Far too often, someone comes to the pastor and complains that something isn't being done, or it isn't being done well enough, so the pastor asks himself, "Who can I count on to make this happen?" He mentally scans the church's terrain and identifies someone who is already doing far too much, but he asks him or her to take on this task too: "I really need you to do this. If you don't, I don't know who will." And far too often, the pastor gives the responsibility to the person he's confident won't say "no": his wife. If this happens too many times, things won't be very pleasant at home! Counting on overworked, overcommitted people may get the job done in the short run, but it almost inevitably has negative long-term effects on everyone involved. We need a more thoughtful, consistent approach to involvement.

The day Connor came to me with his observations, he explained, "We have too few people doing too much in each ministry area. I appreciate all they're doing, but we're not going to get where God wants us to go unless we find a way to involve more people. We can break each role into bite-sized pieces to spread the load and give more people the opportunity to see God use them." He could tell I was tracking with him, so he continued, "If we can get them into the trajectory of church life, they'll realize it's fulfilling to be part of something that's changing lives. Many of them will see opportunities to believe God for more, so they'll take on more challenges and responsibilities. They'll notice problems we don't see, and they'll fix them. They'll notice opportunities we don't see, and they'll step in to take advantage of them. They'll feel great about using their gifts and contributing to the growth of individuals and the church. They'll see themselves as crucial parts of the body of Christ."

I was all in. Connor had put his finger on one of the most important roles of a pastor. He may not have known at that point that many pastors are hesitant to ask people to serve, so when they find someone who is willing to go above and beyond, they don't see that kind of commitment as a problem—they see it as an answer to prayer! Many pastors aren't about to tell overcommitted people to slow down, take a break, or make sure they keep some margin in their lives. Instead, they ask them to do even more because they've proven they're dependable.

When overworked staff members or volunteers eventually crash and burn, pastors too often shake their heads and complain, "Too bad he wasn't faithful for the long haul. I expected more." Those exhausted servants are pushed to the side of the road and left there like a wrecked car. The pastor then finds other eager persons to put in their slots and works them until they too redline and burn out. (This problem wouldn't be so prevalent if more pastors kept from being overcommitted themselves. Then they could see more clearly what was going on in their churches.)

Do you think other people in the church notice this pattern? Of course, they do! That's why they're so reluctant to say "yes" to the pastor's requests to serve. From their point of view, serving in the church only has detrimental effects. It has negative impacts on their schedule, their personal life, their marriage, and their relationships with their kids because family members get only leftovers and sense all the stress. When others witness a few people doing far too much, they make a silent calculus of the costs and conclude their role is to attend and give, but serving isn't an option. Maybe they'll come one day a year for a special day of service, but that's an anomaly.

The New Plan

Connor's plan was to organize each ministry area under him so many more people served in bite-sized chunks of time. For instance, he asked greeters and ushers to form teams that rotated and served only once a month. Some insisted they could do more than that, so Connor asked those people if they wanted to step into a leadership role for one of the teams. He figured out what prompts many more people to say "yes" to an invitation to serve.

Something in human nature, and especially among redeemed people, drives most of us to want to build, create, develop, and inspire others. People want their lives to count, yet they don't want to be trapped in a pastor's unrealistic demands that create too much unrelieved stress with too few benefits. The guilt-driven, unrealistic expectations of many desperate pastors get in the way of their people's God-given desire to contribute and make a difference. We need to inflame their motivation of joyful, grace-driven service and give everybody plenty of on-ramps of involvement.

When involvement in ministry creates more withdrawals than deposits in a person's life, the decline in the account may be gradual or precipitous, but either way, an account balance going in the wrong direction needs to be corrected. Committing to bite-sized responsibility adds to the account, and people become more creative, more responsible, and more excited to take the next step for God to use them. Those people often generate the best ideas for the church because they understand what's going on with newcomers and those who have recently gotten involved, and they can connect with them more effectively. When it's life-giving to them, they invite more people to church, more people come to Christ, and their infectious enthusiasm motivates more people to serve.

Certainly, leaders face large and small crises in leading staff and volunteers (like the ones we addressed in the previous chapter), but we need to create a workable, ongoing plan to recruit, place, train, and encourage as many people as possible to serve God through the church. Some of the ministries are only once a week (greeters, ushers, children's church, etc.). Others, such as caring for those in the hospital, need people every day. And of course, those involved in Sunday services must meet to prepare during the week so the events on Sunday are outstanding.

In everything we do, creating bite-sized roles and on-ramps allow more people to say "yes" to an invitation to serve . . . and to experience the joy of the Lord in their service. The first "yes" leads to more opportunities, more connections with people, and more joy as they see the impact they're having for Christ. When that happens, visitors to church see lots of smiling faces instead of people who look like they've been tortured with sleep deprivation! I don't want people who visit River Valley to leave saying,

"Man, the people at that church sure seem tired and angry." I want them to say, "The people at that church are so warm and welcoming! I can't wait to go back!"

The Transition

To shift to a new model of recruiting and involvement, we need to teach people to think differently about their current roles. In many churches, people have had the same responsibilities for years. Maybe they've made themselves indispensable, or maybe the pastor simply can't find anyone else to take the job. Whatever the case, the person's identity as a human being, as a Christian, and as a leader is often completely wrapped up in that role. Our task is to communicate that every role is a potential stepping stone to something else.

We're all in transition, and when God prompts us, we should be willing to take our tools to another part of the harvest field. I've learned to tell people, "I appreciate so much what you're doing in your current role, but you may be in a different one a year from now. Enjoy what you're doing, and do it with all your heart, but when God prompts you to do something else, don't be surprised. Do it!" I encourage people to dream and pray about where God might lead them next. Gradually, those who serve in our church are learning to listen to the Holy Spirit, eagerly anticipate new challenges, and obey when God gives them new directions. As their pastor, I'm thrilled to see them respond to God in this way!

This open-minded and open-hearted embrace of possible roles is thrilling to some, but it always scares others. If people's reputations are wedded to a role they play, they may not be willing to give it up . . . for any reason. Some of them will wonder if the pastor has concluded they're not doing a good job even though he has thanked them many times in the past. Change rocks the boat, and insecurities and fears spill out. Ironically, those who are most exhausted and burned out are often the most defensive. They may be tired, and they may resent all they've been asked to do, but they can't imagine giving up their primary source of identity.

Ironically, those who are most exhausted and burned out are often the most defensive. They may be tired, and they may resent all they've been asked to do, but they can't imagine giving up their primary source of identity.

Suppose you tell someone you want her to serve in the children's ministry only two weekends a month instead of every Sunday. Even if you explain that you want her to share the load with others so she can go to worship at least half the time, she may think, *So you're saying what I've been doing for the last five years isn't valuable?* Of course you're not saying that, but you shouldn't be surprised when you get pushback of every sort. Let me offer a few suggestions:

An apology

I think it's entirely appropriate for pastors to apologize to the people who have shouldered too much of the load. The pastor might say, "I've learned some things about leadership and delegation, and it's time we made some changes. I'm so sorry that I've asked you to do so much for so long. You've done a great job, but I don't think it's been the best thing for you, and I haven't given other people the opportunity to serve like they want to. I need your help in making this transition. Let's fix this together. Will you help me?"

Be ruthlessly realistic

We have a big vision, and we hope people catch it and dive in to follow us in doing great things for God. The problem is that our plans can be so much bigger than our resources, so we put too much of the burden on too few people. In an article for *Christianity Today*, Pastor Karl Vaters observes that "too many churches of 50 are trying to do all the activities of a church of 500." This, he rightly asserts, is unhealthy for everybody. He explains his approach:

> When we adapt our methods to suit our size, we discover that a lot of things we thought were essential aren't so essential any more. For instance, when 20 or fewer people show up for a meeting, there's no need to line them up in rows, speak through a microphone, have a band lead in worship or offer multiple levels of age-appropriate child care. Maybe the best way to do church at that size is to form the chairs in a circle. Talk, pray and sing together. Do some Q & A. Make it more about dialog than monolog.[9]

Smaller churches need to do a few things really well instead of trying to do a wide range of things well without the resources to pull it off. They need to tailor their programs to the available leadership and the volunteers needed to make their programs excellent. Some programs will have to wait until the church is bigger and there are more leaders in the mix.

Carefully communicate the plan

When I talked to a large audience at our church about making some changes, I explained the concept and anticipated their emotional response by describing, "You probably feel . . ." When I went through the litany of possible reactions, people felt understood—which is very important in helping them own the changes. On the range of responses, a few jumped on board immediately and wondered why it took me so long; many needed to ask some questions and get answers before they could feel comfortable with the changes; and some people were genuinely resistant. They couldn't imagine what had come over me that I'd shake up their lives by asking them to consider that God may call them to do something else. I even joked that the sound guys probably booby trapped the system so they can never be replaced!

When I shared this strategy with the staff and ministry leaders in our church, some of them said, "You don't understand. I've asked people to serve. I've pleaded with them, taught them, and tried to make it as easy as possible, but I end up with a few doing a lot and many doing little or nothing. They believe that if they say 'yes,' they'll never have a life again."

I had to explain again and again that we wanted to give as many people as possible the opportunity to say "yes" so they could thrive in their roles. But every commitment is short-term. They may be fulfilling a very different role in the future. No one is trapped. No one is expected to die from exhaustion. No one should lose their family because they spend too much time serving at the church, and others should discover the joy of living by finding an appropriate place to serve God and others. A "yes" means they're making a commitment to touch lives in meaningful ways, playing a part—a small part—in being an integral component of the body of Christ, and caring for people in the church and the community. As they use their gifts to the glory of God, they'll grow in their effectiveness and their love for God. When God prompts them to do something else or something more, that's fantastic! It's our job to help them find the sweet spot for this season of their walk with Christ.

Address the awkwardness

All change is threatening. Some people thrive on the exhilaration, but most need comfort and encouragement as the process unfolds. When pastors create easy on-ramps, they need to accentuate the joy of serving, not the obligation—the *beauty* of the King of the universe involving others in His divine work instead of merely their *duty* to fill a slot or do what the pastor has asked them to do. We want people to join God in the grandest enterprise the world has ever known, to build His Church, and we want them to come with joy as they anticipate all God will do.

When pastors create easy on-ramps, they need to accentuate the joy of serving, not the obligation—the *beauty* of the King of the universe involving others in His divine work instead of merely their *duty* to fill a slot or do what the pastor has asked them to do.

I reassured the congregation that I was committed to protect them by not asking them to serve on too many teams. I promised I would invite everyone to serve, but we would also ask some people to step back if we sensed they were already doing too much.

I'm sure some wondered if I was telling the truth or just blowing smoke, but word got around pretty fast when I backed up that promise with conversations to help people find the role that best fit their gifts, their passions, and their availability.

During our church's transition, many people were thrilled, but I also heard some complaints: "I thought we paid *you* to do all this." I wondered what was behind those comments. Some people, I realized, had never been actively involved in serving at a church, and they assumed that staff positions existed so the rest of the people could come, soak in the teaching, and go home. I know this is a common misconception because a number of people who have joined our church have told me, "I've been going to church for decades, but I had no idea I was supposed to serve. I thought it was all up to you and the staff." They would vote for board members they presumed would help the staff pull off all the programs in the church. I think it's easy for people to believe their giving earns them the right to watch, expecting those who don't give (at least as much) to feel obligated to serve. There may have been other motives for their complaints, but these probably covered most of the particular objections.

I realized I needed to do a better job of communicating the roles of the pastor, the staff, the board, and the ministry leaders. It's not the staff's job to do all the work of ministry. Our job is to equip everyone to play the parts God has gifted them to perform. We are responsible to guide people where they can serve most joyfully and effectively, and to protect them from burnout from carrying too much responsibility and putting in too many hours. Leaders don't just recruit, place, and forget about team members until they mess up so badly that we need to get involved. Instead, we recruit, listen, place, and protect people so they thoroughly enjoy serving the Lord. Obedience today is an open door to more opportunities tomorrow.

Obedience today is an open door to more opportunities tomorrow.

Service roles are like monkey bars. Many people grab the first one and never let go (or never are allowed to let go). Instead, I want people to see the next bar, grab it, let go of the last one, grab the next one, let go, and on and on. If people try to grab the next one but aren't willing to let go of the last one, they get stuck. Action on the monkey bars is fun and exhilarating. That's the way I want people to feel when they're involved in our church.

A more flexible strategy for involvement sometimes brings hidden fears to the surface. For instance, when we tell a childcare worker she will only be serving two Sundays a month so she can attend worship, or to serve at one service and go to another one, her pushback may be a signal that deeper issues need to be resolved. She may be more comfortable with children than adults; she may be hiding in the nursery because she doesn't feel qualified to serve anywhere else; or she may have other reservations. When people are resistant, it's a good time to stop, ask tender but pertinent questions, and listen. Quite often, this conversation uncovers long-buried hurts and fears. It can be one of the most positive, healing, transformational talks we can have with someone who is resistant . . . but only if the goal is pastoring the person instead of filling empty slots on the organizational chart.

A culture of open choices in ministry is much more fluid that just filling positions to get jobs done. We never know how God might lead someone, and we never know how God might lead us to ask someone to be involved in a different role. In this environment, it's not *either* the individual's sense of leading *or* a leader's need to ask someone to play an important role. Those aren't mutually exclusive. It's both/and. We want people to pray and ask God to lead them, and we tell our leaders to invite people to join their teams. Somewhere in the middle of all that, people find a meaningful role and a supportive team . . . until the next one comes along.

Encouraging signs

The transition to a new culture of serving takes a while. I can tell people get it when we ask them to join a team and take a responsibility and they don't look terrified because they know the role is temporary (they aren't trapped), and we're protecting them (it's a bite-sized job). I also know people get it when they're happy to serve one or two Sundays a month instead of every week, and too, when individuals tell their ministry leader, "I think I'm ready for something more. Will you help me find a role with more responsibility?" I've seen many people serve in a Sunday role, as a greeter or usher or in the children's ministry, but who then ask if they can lead a Life Group. It allows them to lead their group each week, and they serve in the worship service once a month. That's a perfect fit for many people.

The pastor's role in the transition

For our church to make a cultural shift in how we involved people, I had to patiently and persistently reeducate our ministry leaders. Most of them immediately saw the benefits of the transition, and they jumped on board. Even then, they had plenty of questions about the specific applications in their areas of church life.

When I talked to the congregation, I explained the concept of the body of Christ. We are each part of the whole, but we play distinct parts, as Paul explained:

> Just as a body, though one, has many parts, but all its many parts form one body, so it is with Christ. For we were all baptized by one Spirit so as to form one body—whether Jews or Gentiles, slave or free—and we were all given the one Spirit to drink. Even so the body is not made up of one part but of many (1 Corinthians 12:12-14).

It's not all about the pastor. God wants every believer to step up and play a role. The roles may be very different, but all are crucial. The body suffers if each person doesn't do his or her part. In fact, the roles that seem most obscure are the most important:

> The eye cannot say to the hand, "I don't need you!" And the head cannot say to the feet, "I don't need you!" On the contrary, those parts of the body that seem to be weaker are indispensable, and the parts that we think are less honorable we treat with special honor. And the parts that are unpresentable are treated with special modesty, while our presentable parts need no special treatment. But God has put the body together, giving greater honor to the parts that lacked it, so that there should be no division in the body, but that its parts should have equal concern for each other. If one part suffers, every part

suffers with it; if one part is honored, every part rejoices with it (1 Corinthians 12:21-26).

To apply this biblical principle specifically to our church, our team described the ministries of our church and how we wanted people to fill bite-sized roles for a while, in most cases a year or two. To show that we wanted everyone involved, I gave numeric goals for each ministry—and they were big numbers. I explained that we weren't just filling slots; we wanted people who served to experience joy and fulfillment. We gave everyone time to ask

---

Churches don't grow strong only because of terrific preaching and teaching. They grow bigger, deeper, and stronger as glad volunteers go to work.

---

questions and sign up, and then we celebrated like mad when so many did.

When more people are involved—and love being involved— fantastic things happen. Churches don't grow strong only because of terrific preaching and teaching. They grow bigger, deeper, and stronger as glad volunteers go to work. Samuel R. Chand is a leadership consultant, my personal coach, and a good friend. He has observed that for every new volunteer a church recruits and places, the church grows by four people. When I attended a pastors' conference on church growth, he asked participants to tell him the number of people in attendance each week in their churches and the number of volunteers. With remarkable consistency, the relationship came out very close to four to one. His conclusion was that if we want our churches to grow, we need to invest our hearts, minds, and time in strategies that multiply our volunteers.

I believe he's absolutely right. For years, we prayed for growth at River Valley, but we didn't grow as fast because we didn't have enough volunteers to serve more people. We had a large front door, but too many visitors left through the back door because we didn't have enough meaningful touches when they were with us.

When people come to our churches for the first time, they often bring deeply rooted and sometimes very odd expectations based on their previous experiences. Becca and I invited some new neighbors who had two young children to visit our church. Before they agreed to come, the wife asked, "Will we need to serve in the children's ministry if we come to church here?"

Becca wasn't sure she understood her, so she asked, "What do you mean?"

The woman explained, "We went to a church last week, but there was nobody working in the nursery. The pastor said that if we wanted our kids to be in the nursery, we'd have to stay there with them. We weren't sure what to do, so we agreed to stay there. Soon, other parents brought their kids to us. We were visitors, yet the pastor put us in charge of the nursery. I wanted to know if that's what you will expect us to do."

"No, no, no!" Becca jumped in. "You don't have to do that at our church! We have wonderful people in charge of our nursery and children's ministry. We want first-time visitors to be able to check their kids in and go to the worship service. The kids will have a great time and be ready when you go back to pick them up. No, you don't have to be in charge of the nursery at River Valley Church." Our neighbor looked relieved, so Becca continued, "Someday, you might want to serve in the nursery or somewhere else in the church, but if so, you'll be on a team that serves only a few Sundays a month. No hurry and no pressure, but when and if you'd like to do something like that, you can." Our neighbors started attending, and the really neat thing is that the wife now serves faithfully in our Gokids ministry and her husband is on the ushering team!

I want to jump on the pastor who asked this couple to be in charge of the nursery when they were first-time visitors, but I have to admit I made more than my share of similar blunders when I was a sugar pastor. I used people to get jobs done, celebrated their commitment as they burned out instead of protecting them, and quickly moved on to find someone else to fill the slots. I was redlining, and I thought it was perfectly okay to expect others to give until they were utterly exhausted. I didn't empower the members of Christ's body to serve with joy and power; I disempowered people by raising expectations and giving them too few resources and encouragement.

If you happen to be one of those people who suffered under my leadership, please accept my apology. I have shared it from the pulpit, but let me put it in print: I'm sorry for doing that to you or any of your friends. And if you read this and you felt used and discarded by the pastor of another church, please accept my apology on behalf of Christ and His body. Serving Jesus might tire you out at times, but it should be life giving!

Where Now?

When I planted the church, I needed people to serve. I felt the pressure, so I pressured others to shoulder the load with me. I believed that was just the way churches operated. As my perspective has shifted, I now realize that my motive to get people to serve is that they will experience more of God's joy if they find roles that maximize their gifts, if they see results in changed lives, and if they serve on a team of joyful, dedicated people who understand that a bite-sized responsibility is exactly right for each of them. I no longer want people to serve primarily to make my life easier by meeting a need in the church. I want them to serve because it's best for them, their walks with God, their sense of purpose, and the impact they can have on others.

If you're planting a church or your church has too few volunteers, recruit and place the best people you can find, but assure them, "I'm not going to let you crash and burn. I want you to find people to join your team so you all have a bite-sized responsibility." As long as a role doesn't require a background check (as in the case of anyone working with kids in our church), our ministry leaders don't have to get permission to ask someone to join their teams. The best leaders are always looking for men and women who are available. They may not fit in that particular role for a long time, but for a while, they get their feet wet in ministry.

Pastors should probably assess their volunteer strategy every quarter to determine which teams are flourishing and which seem to be struggling. The problem isn't always impure motives or disobedience. The chief problems we address every quarter are the holes created by mobility. About fifteen percent of our people move or move on in a given year, so about fifteen percent of the volunteers need to be replaced. We ask our Life Team leaders: Is the system working, or do we need to talk about the strategy and motivation to remind people why we do what we do? If it needs attention, do I need to speak from the platform on the privilege to serve, do we do a video, or should the message come through the ministry leaders?

We tell our ministry leaders to become skilled at "shoulder tapping," that is, tapping people on the shoulder and saying, "I'd love for you to join me in this ministry. Will you?" One of the ushers in our church took me up on this. Before Easter one year, he invited a friend who didn't know Jesus to join him in ushering. He explained, "Our church will be packed on Easter. I'm an usher, and I could really use your help seating people and taking up the offering."

His friend immediately said, "Hey, if you need me, I'm there!"

All during the service, the new guy followed directions and did his job really well. At the end of the service, I gave a gospel presentation and asked people to raise their hands if they were ready to receive forgiveness and say yes to Jesus. I looked over the congregation, and I saw an usher with his hand raised. I ignored him because I thought, *Who trained that guy? Usher guy doesn't even know he's not supposed to raise his hand!* But as I acknowledged people all around the room, he still had his hand raised. I ignored him again. The next time my eyes went in his direction, I saw that he was now pointing to himself—he didn't want me to miss him again! Finally, I realized he was serious. I said, "I see that hand," but I wondered what in the world this usher was doing. The man's wife was sitting on the front row with his friend's wife. Of course, I didn't put the two together since I'd never seen either of them before, but his wife had also raised her hand to receive Christ. Our usher had invited a neighbor to join him in serving, and two people had entered God's kingdom as a result. "Usher guy" will always have a place of honor in the story of our church, and I'm so glad his friend tapped his shoulder and asked for help!

If you're a pastor, make this transition. It's too important to wait any longer. Everyone will be healthier and happier if you do.

If you're serving in a church, find a bite-sized role that fits your talents, passions, and time. Don't feel guilty that you aren't doing more. Find your sense of identity and value in the One who loved you before you did anything to please Him, while you were His enemy. His love isn't based on how much you do for Him; it's unconditional. Actually, it's counter-conditional, in spite of your performance! Bask in His grace, love, and power, and serve Him with unbridled joy. As you do, I'm sure you'll grow into the next place of serving and leadership and do it with a smile on your face as you make an eternal difference.

Think about it:

1. How would you describe the concept of giving people a "bite-sized" role? What problems does it solve? What problems does it create?

2. What are some differences between recruiting and placing people to fill a slot in a crisis and crafting a carefully planned strategy to enlist, place, train, and encourage people in specific roles with limited demands and an open door to other opportunities?

3. What are some issues pastors face during the awkward transition from the old strategy of recruiting and placing volunteers to the new one? How would you address each one?

4. What are the current strengths of your volunteer strategy? Based on the principles in this chapter, what are some things you could improve?

5. How will you communicate that the heart of serving comes from joyful obedience, not merely meeting demands to get a job done?

CHAPTER 6

SHORTEN THE PIPELINE

I never intended for River Valley to be a multi-site church. I planned to keep building as we kept growing. As we outgrew each facility, we'd find bigger tracts of land and build larger auditoriums. In 2007, we averaged more than 1200 people each Sunday and we were bursting at the seams. I knew the next move would set the direction for our church for many years . . . and potentially involve many millions of dollars. I had recently talked to a pastor whose church spent $20 million on a new building. That's a lot of money, and I didn't want to mess up this decision! I desperately wanted to hear from God, so I went on a two-day prayer retreat. I drove about an hour from home and checked into a hotel room.

As I prayed, I sensed the Holy Spirit's leading for our church to go multi-site. I didn't want to hear that. I argued: "God, that strategy won't work in Minnesota. It may work in other parts of the country, but not here." I prayed more, listening intently for a different message from God. I didn't get one. Instead, the Spirit confirmed several times that He wanted River Valley to plant additional churches instead of building bigger and bigger buildings.

Continuing to pray, I felt that God wanted me to get a map of the state, so I went to a nearby store to get one. When I got back to the room, I unfolded the map and taped it to the wall. The Holy Spirit often gives directions only for the very next step, and He wants us to trust Him with fresh dependence at each new step, but this was different. As I looked at the map, I felt the Spirit tell me, "Put a Post-It note on that city." "Put one on that town." "Put one here too." By the time He was finished, there were nine Post-It notes on the map.

I stepped back and looked at the map. I was excited, but I was also a bit skeptical. Had I really heard from God, or was all this just auto-suggestion? At that moment, I sensed God break through: "To prove to you that going multi-site is My will, I'm going to give you a building in one of those cities." Talk about a fleece!

I went home excited that God had spoken so clearly. In our next staff meeting, I announced that the direction of our church was to plant additional churches and go multi-site instead of building larger and larger buildings. My staff knew very well that's not what I had wanted to do, so they were curious. I explained, "God is going to prove this is His will by giving us a building." Okay, it was out on the table. I was all in. Now it was entirely up to God.

The next day, our denominational superintendent called me and asked, "Pastor Rob, have you ever thought of your church being multi-site?"

I'm sure I was smiling. "Well, actually, I told our team yesterday that I believe that's God's leading."

"A church in a town near you wants to give someone their building."

I asked, "Where is it?"

"Fairbault."

I screamed into the phone, "I put a Post-It note on Fairbault, Minnesota!" I'm quite sure he didn't understand the significance of that information. Fairbault is about thirty-five minutes south of Minneapolis, but I had never been there. I explained that God had led me in prayer to identify the town as one of the places where He wants our church to have a presence.

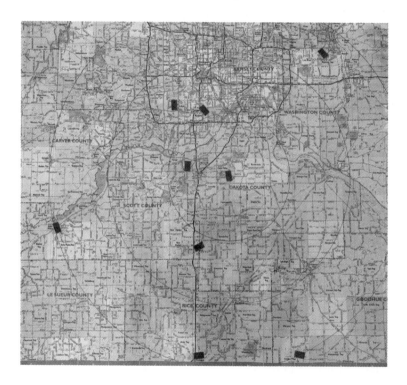

The decision to establish multi-site churches forced us to reevaluate how we develop leaders. If we were going to produce strong satellite campuses, we certainly couldn't wing it, and we couldn't throw a bunch of loosely related strategies at those churches and hope one of them was effective. Developing outstanding leaders became a core value and a high priority for River Valley. If we wanted all of our campuses to thrive, we had to create a workable leadership development strategy and system. We couldn't depend on the pastors to fix all the problems. You can't build a great church without a large number of "them" fixing problems. In multiplying competent and godly "thems," we couldn't afford to fail.

Pastors need a great strategy to get people involved as soon as possible. At River Valley, we've worked hard to shorten the leadership pipeline. We reach out into the community, share the gospel, lead people to faith in Christ, equip them, and release them to make a difference in our church and in their world.

Three Components

A leadership pipeline has three parts: a wide funnel of recruitment at the start, effective equipping in the middle, and ready opportunities to serve as people are trained and released. Each step is essential. The pastor needs to communicate this strategy as the new normal. It's how God gathers His people, prepares them, and uses them for His glory.

All believers are on a mission for God. In his first letter, The Apostle Peter made a remarkable statement about the radical nature of the church. We aren't just another human institution that tries to do good and help people. Yes, we're that, but we're so much more. Peter's letter echoes something God said centuries earlier. Before God gave Moses the Ten Commandments, He told Moses to tell the people, "You yourselves have seen what I did to Egypt, and how I carried you on eagles' wings and brought you to myself. Now if you obey me fully and keep my covenant, then out of all nations you will be my treasured possession. Although the whole earth is mine, you will be for me a kingdom of priests and a holy nation" (Exodus 19:4-6).

Of course, God's people didn't obey Him fully and keep His covenant. Far from it. Much of the rest of the Old Testament is the sad story of their indifference and rebellion, but even in their darkest days, God didn't give up on them. He promised to send a Savior—one who obeyed God fully, who did what we couldn't do, and paid the price we should have paid for our sins. When we trust in Jesus, we don't just change our schedule for an hour on Sunday mornings. We take on a new relationship with God, and we have a new status that radically affects every aspect of our lives, 24/7.

This brings us back to Peter's letter. He wrote, "But you are a chosen people, a royal priesthood, a holy nation, God's special possession, that you may declare the praises of him who called you out of darkness into his wonderful light. Once you were not a people, but now you are the people of God; once you had not received mercy, but now you have received mercy" (1 Peter 2:9-10).

Does that sound familiar? It should. Christ totally fulfilled the covenant. He is the sacrifice, the high priest, the King, and the source of truth. Because we are "in him," Peter says that *we* are royal, *we* are priests, and *we* are prophets who "declare the praises of him who called [us] out of darkness into his wonderful light."

To whom do we declare these praises? To each other, certainly, but also to everyone on the planet. At Pentecost when the Holy Spirit came down and rested on the 120 disciples as tongues of fire, they immediately went out and told people about the wonder of God's grace. The Holy Spirit still prompts disciples to do the same thing. We are new people, radically changed in our status, our relationships, and our motivations. And God has entrusted His mission to each of us—not just pastors, but to every person who claims Christ as Savior.

Decades after Pentecost, Paul had traveled throughout the Roman world telling everyone who would listen (and many who wouldn't) about Jesus. No matter how often he was beaten, stoned, imprisoned, whipped, and despised for his faith, he never lost his passion to tell people about the saving love of Christ. Near the end of his letter to the Colossians, he asks them to join him in trusting God to open doors for the gospel:

> Devote yourselves to prayer, being watchful and thankful. And pray for us, too, that God may open a door for our message, so that we may proclaim the mystery of Christ, for which I am in chains. Pray that I may proclaim it clearly, as I should. Be wise in the way you act toward outsiders; make the most of every opportunity. Let your conversation be always full of grace, seasoned with salt, so that you may know how to answer everyone (Colossians 4:2-6).

The door God opens is often to speak to our neighbors next door, but He wants our hearts to break for every person, especially those who have nothing to offer us in return.

The door God opens is often to speak to our neighbors next door, but He wants our hearts to break for every person, especially those who have nothing to offer us in return. Jesus told a parable about a wedding feast, and He concluded by telling the host, "When you give a luncheon or dinner, do not invite your friends, your brothers or sisters, your relatives, or your rich neighbors; if you do, they may invite you back and so you will be repaid. But when you give a banquet, invite the poor, the crippled, the lame, the blind, and you will be blessed. Although they cannot repay you, you will be repaid at the resurrection of the righteous" (Luke 14:12-14).

Our goal is to fill the banquet table with people who hear the message of God's grace and respond in faith. Evangelism isn't limited to the pastor's job description. If people have experienced grace, they want to share it with others. If they've found hope, they want others to find it too. If they've found security in a relationship with the God of the universe, they want others to find Him faithful too. And they don't devote only leftover time and resources in a halfhearted effort to reach people with the gospel. Each believer invests time, creativity, resources, and hearts in people who need a Savior. Wise leaders realize that if our people aren't full and overflowing with the grace of God, they haven't experienced enough of it to matter to them.

As people respond to Christ and become part of His body, our role is to give them assurance, stability, and a vision for how God might use them. Quite often, the very best evangelists are new believers because they're excited, and they have a lot of friends who aren't believers. Even when people have been Christians for years, they can learn to be culturally relevant and socially astute. We never cram the gospel down anyone's throat. As Peter described, we tell them how God has called us out of darkness into His wonderful light, and we let them decide how to respond. We're not at all surprised when they don't respond right away. Most people need plenty of questions answered, consistent friendship, and lots of time before they make a decision that will affect every aspect of their lives for eternity. We give them room to wrestle with the truth and its implications, and we love them no matter how they respond.

In the middle phase of the leadership pipeline, once someone says yes to Jesus as their Lord and Savior, we conduct training and provide opportunities for them to try different ministries inside and outside the church's walls. Some people call this training "discipleship," others call it "spiritual formation." It involves teaching the basics of the Christian life like prayer, Bible study, and small group involvement; it helps them identify their spiritual gifts; and it offers direction for involvement during and after the training. At River Valley we have a class we call Next. (After people say yes to Jesus and ask, "What's next?" we invite them to this class!)

When people come out of this part of the pipeline, we need to make their transition to serving absolutely seamless. We're constantly trying to improve this, and our goal is to get it right every time. If they come out excited and motivated, but no one connects with them to offer an opportunity to serve, their excitement quickly fades. And the connection isn't only about a role in the church. Ministry leaders begin real relationships with these people; they become partners, friends, coaches, and cheerleaders.

As I explained in the last chapter, we make sure people know that every role is temporary, and we assure them they won't be trapped as they grow and desire more challenge. If they love it, they may move into a leadership role when the time is right. If they don't feel fulfilled in that role, the ministry leaders help them find one that fits better. No one is treated with even a hint of disdain if they want to move to a different role, and all of us are thrilled when people find the sweet spot in serving the Lord.

In a *Harvard Business Review* article on five crucial elements of a leadership pipeline, Josh Bersin asserts that an effective model in the corporate world produces multiplied benefits. He cites examples of companies that . . .

> . . . believe in matrix management and risk taking—both attributes are highly predictive of long-term revenue per employee and gross profit margin. A matrixed organization forces leaders to collaborate beyond boundaries. To be effective, they must build networks, move from role to role, and build depth of understanding across the business. Leaders' growth in these areas leads to enduring growth for the enterprise.

Bersin's research shows that organizations that follow the model he recommends "bring in 37% more revenue per employee, are four times more likely to be efficient (measured through profitability), and are three times more likely to be the market leader and innovative by nature than the low performers" he studied.[10]

Of course, the payoff for churches is somewhat different than for businesses, but the point is clear: this study shows that effective leaders have the courage to take risks in assigning responsibilities and are flexible in moving people to roles where they can serve and grow. Our goal should be to get people into the places where God designed them to thrive.

The Heart of Leadership

Our church has a comprehensive strategy and materials we use for each part of the pipeline, but another aspect is just as crucial. For this process to work well, pastors need to acknowledge: "This isn't *my* church. It's *God's* church."

I understand that pastors regularly use the term "my church," and that's perfectly fine if they're distinguishing where they serve from other churches. The point I'm making isn't a matter of semantics in a conversation at a pastors' conference. It's a question of ownership and honor: Are we excited when God uses highly competent people to do amazing things, or are we so threatened that we consciously or subconsciously don't want to hire staff and create a pipeline that produces people who excel in ministry? At that point, it's not about strategy; it's about pride and humility. Just as we tell people they are in a temporary place of service and God will probably move them to a different role as they grow, pastors need to see themselves in a temporary role. When God speaks to move them, they need to be quick to listen and obey.

A leadership pipeline is created to empower God's people to fulfill *His* purposes by doing *His* work in *His* way to build *His* church.

A leadership pipeline is created to empower God's people to fulfill *His* purposes by doing *His* work in *His* way to build *His* church. When we use words like "my" and "mine" too often, it may say something about our hearts. The scorecard shouldn't reflect who is praising our leadership, but rather who is praising God for the wonder of His grace and power. And we shouldn't be as concerned about how many people are in our seats as with how many are motivated to serve God with all their hearts and follow Him wherever He leads them.

The mission of our church is to train them all, keep some, and send the rest. This means I don't "own" River Valley Church; it's God's. And our church doesn't "own" the people who come through our doors; the kingdom of God is far, far bigger than River Valley (or your church). I told the men and women in our internship program, "Although it breaks our hearts to train so many talented people that we don't have room for in our church, we're thrilled to send them out and see them follow God into another part of the harvest field. We may lead them to Jesus, pastor them, and train them, but they're Christ's disciples, not ours."

I'm well aware that a lot of pastors don't think this way . . . because I didn't either, for a long time. A lot of us are giving everything we've got to attract people and keep the churches solvent. We're spinning so many plates that adding a comprehensive leadership pipeline seems like a bridge too far. It's easy, it's natural to be competitive and defensive about the size of our churches, but that perspective kills us.

When we set our eyes on personal success rather than honoring God, we cease to serve Him. Instead, we use Him to accomplish our purposes of success, power, and approval. At the end of the biblical era of the judges, God's people looked around and saw that every other nation had a king, and they wanted one too. God warned them that it was a bad decision, but they insisted. God gave them Saul as their first king. He was a mixed bag: bold and timid, wise and foolish.

The prophet Samuel spoke God's word to him over and over, and finally, he gave Saul God's very clear instructions: "I am the one the Lord sent to anoint you king over his people Israel; so listen now to the message from the Lord. This is what the Lord Almighty says: 'I will punish the Amalekites for what they did to Israel when they waylaid them as they came up from Egypt. Now go, attack the Amalekites and totally destroy all that belongs to them'" (1 Samuel 15:1-3).

Saul led the army into victorious battle, but he didn't obey God's directions. He spared the life of Agag, king of the Amalekites, and he kept the finest livestock. When Samuel confronted him, Saul wimped out. He tried to convince Samuel that he had obeyed God (well, mostly!), and he blamed his soldiers for saving the best of the livestock. It's easy to shake our heads at Saul and think, *I'd never do anything like that!* Oh really? How often do we choose what's convenient or reasonable over God's clear directions? How much do we compare our numbers to those of other pastors, leaders, and churches? How often do we love the approval of men more than the approval of God? If we ask the Holy Spirit to reveal what's in our hearts, I think all of us will find some reasons to repent.

When I challenge pastors to listen to the voice of God and obey Him in building leaders for the kingdom, a lot of them tell me they're afraid they'll be fired. They assume people in their churches, and even people on their boards, don't want their pastor to train them to serve. They want a good sermon, a hospital visit when they need one, and effective programs for their kids. They don't want to expend any more energy, they don't want to be stretched, and they don't want to feel the least bit uncomfortable. They want to be entertained and hang out with their friends, so when the pastor tells them God has given their church a mission to reach their city and the world, they push back (or vanish). The pastors who make this assumption may be right, but maybe not. If they're right, they have two options: clearly and boldly teach their people about God's calling for every Christian to a radical commitment . . . or leave that church and plant one with the DNA of God's kingdom from the first day. I tell them, "Whatever you do, don't live in fear and don't be stagnant. Know God's call in your life, listen to Him, patiently teach the truth about who we are and what God has called us to do, and equip all who are willing to join you in the Great Commission. Nothing less and nothing else."

When a human body is diseased and shutting down, blood flow is reduced to the extremities and directed to the vital organs. Gradually, other systems shut down and the blood is concentrated on only the heart and lungs. This is a picture of a lot of churches: a diseased church concentrates its energy on only a few vital people, and the extremities (the rest of the people) spiritually die from a lack of nourishment and movement. The body only thrives when life-giving blood goes to every cell, from the earlobes to the toenails. We can't accomplish what God has called us to do if we try to do it alone or only with a handful of tired laborers. We need every person in the body of Christ to sense God's heart, listen to His voice, and engage in His mission.

On a microscopic scale, the human body is continually replenishing itself with new cells. Each part has its predictable life cycle. The lining of the stomach is continually in contact with acid, so those cells are replaced every few days, but bone cells take about ten years to be replaced.[11] Scientists now know that neurons in the brain aren't ever replaced—we have the same ones from the day we're born until we die. Red blood cells stay busy taking oxygen and nutrients to every cell in the body. About 100 million new ones are created every minute.[12] From such medical observations, we can make two applications: each person in the body of Christ needs to be continually refreshed with God's grace and truth to stay strong and healthy, and on a larger scale, we can expect a "churn" of people who play particular roles in the church as some leave and are replaced by others. If pastors anticipate a natural process of replacement, they'll continually reach out to share the gospel and lead people to Christ, empower them through training and teaching, and send them to play crucial roles in the life of the body. If they assume the people they have today are the ones they'll have tomorrow, they'll be frustrated when people leave positions, they'll use guilt to get people to stay, and they won't do a good job at any of the three sections of the leadership pipeline.

Next Steps

Some churches have outstanding outreach activities, but they don't do much to disciple people and equip them to serve. Other churches teach in-depth spiritual growth classes, but they don't do much evangelism, and people often sit in those classes for years without serving. All three parts of the pipeline are crucial; the system fails if we omit any of them.

I've heard some pastors who have a heart for evangelism, but not for lost people. Does that sound strange? Let me explain. When I listen to them preach the gospel, it feels like they're talking at "those people." They want to convert them so they'll be acceptable to the people in the church. That's not how Jesus related to people outside the family of God! The Pharisees had contempt for sinners, but Jesus was amazingly kind, tender, and gracious to the outcasts and misfits of His society. He treated a Samaritan woman with respect, stopped to connect with a sick woman to let her know His power to heal was coupled with genuine love for her, and I'm sure laughed with delight as four guys lowered their paralyzed buddy through the roof right in front of Jesus so He could heal him. It seems Jesus was especially happy to heal people on the Sabbath, which infuriated the legalistic religious elite!

How well do we speak the language of people who aren't in God's family? What words do we use to label them? What is the tone in our voice when we speak of those who are from "a far country"?

How well do we speak the language of people who aren't in God's family? What words do we use to label them? What is the tone in our voice when we speak of those who are from "a far country"? Do we genuinely love them like Jesus did, or do we consider them as problems to be solved or projects to be accomplished? It matters . . . it matters a lot. We're asking people to change their hearts about God, and if our hearts aren't filled with love for them, our asking rings hollow, or worse, manipulative.

Let me recommend two very specific steps pastors can take. First, give gospel presentations in church, and ask for a response— hands raised or walking down the aisle—a public display of a commitment to Jesus. If you haven't asked for a response for a while, do it this week. I do this in about half of the services, but other pastors on our team ask for responses every week. When I make this recommendation, some pastors ask, "But Pastor Rob, what if nobody responds? What if there's nothing at all?" I tell them, "That's fine, no problem, but I'd end the service by praying, 'Lord Jesus, I don't want to pastor a church that doesn't have people trust You as their Savior. I pray for the people in our congregation that they would invite their friends to church next week so when I share the gospel, their friends will trust in You." Hopefully that lets everyone know you want to see people come to faith in Jesus!

The second recommendation is to speak to the people in the congregation as if they had all brought their unbelieving friends. This means we don't use insider jargon, we don't sing odd songs, and we don't communicate about "those people" with even a hint of contempt. Instead, we meet people where they are, not expecting them to know anything about the Bible. In our messages to everyone in the congregation, we "backfill the story," explaining who, where, when, why, and how as if we were talking only to people who are unfamiliar with the Bible. For instance, if I'm reading a Gospel passage about Peter or from one of Peter's letters, I'll say, "Peter is one of Jesus' followers. In fact, many people consider him to be the leader of His followers. There were twelve that Jesus picked and called 'apostles,' and Jesus trained them for three years. The passage in the Bible we're reading about Peter says: . . ."

In other words, don't make any assumptions about what people know and understand. (Even as I write this book, I want to backfill every biblical reference, but I'm assuming readers will be pastors, church leaders, or growing volunteers who have some basic Bible knowledge.)

This approach has two significant benefits. First, many people in church don't know the background of the people and the situations, so they'll learn something important. And second, they'll think, *Hey, I can invite my non-Christian neighbor to come, and he won't be freaked out by church!* Those are two excellent outcomes.

During sermon preparation, we might envision a group of unbelievers sitting in the front row. How would we talk to them in their living rooms? How patient would we be to make sure they understand words and concepts that are undoubtedly unfamiliar to them? What are their preconceptions about God . . . and just as important, their preconceptions about church people and pastors? Do they see Christians as judgmental Pharisees or as compassionate followers of Jesus? What's the best way to gently challenge and correct their preconceptions?

Through our messages, we can enter our listeners' mental and emotional landscape and say, "You may be thinking . . ." or "When you hear this verse, you're probably feeling . . ." Most of us will need to make a dramatic shift in our preaching and teaching to direct our messages to the ears of those who don't know Christ, but it will pay incredible dividends in the life of the church. Some people who attend other churches in our area have told me they wanted their neighbors to hear about Jesus, so they brought them to our church because they realized we relate better to people who aren't yet in the family of God. I'm glad they know that about us and I pray that other churches grow in this awareness.

Our evangelism strategy is both "come and see" and "go and tell." We want our people to be excited about bringing their neighbors and friends to church to hear the message of forgiveness and restoration, but we also encourage them to be light and salt in every relationship at home, at work, and in the community.

If we're sensitive, gracious, and clear in our gospel presentations on Sunday mornings, our people are more likely to be sensitive, gracious, and clear when they sit down over coffee with a friend or neighbor.

When people trust in Christ in one of our services, we point them to a prayer team member, an usher, or the welcome center where someone connects personally with them and gives them a *Now What?* resource book. We provide information about reading the Bible, prayer, and resources at the church, and we invite them to our four-week Next class so we can help them grow in their new faith and find out more about our church. The class covers everything they need to start on firm footing: assurance of salvation, the role of the Holy Spirit, a spiritual gifts inventory, baptism, small groups, and opportunities to become involved in the life of the church. At the end of this class, we find out how people want to serve in the church or in an outreach, and we give them an opportunity to join a team.

After Next, we invite newcomers to join one of our Alpha classes. These have been used by churches around the world, and they are very effective in grounding people in their faith. The Alpha classes lead directly to ongoing Life Groups, our small group ministry.

Each of these transitions poses a danger of people falling through the cracks, so we don't just give them information and hope they find their way to the next thing. We try to have a smooth, gracious handoff from one activity to the next, with the leader of the first class helping them connect with the leader of the next one. It takes time, diligence, and patience, but it's well worth the effort so people feel valued and connected.

A Short Runway to Service

Our strategy is to involve people quickly in serving and then trust the ministry leaders to give them adequate training. The youth pastor trains the new youth leaders who sign up, our Life Groups pastor trains the new group leaders, and on and on throughout the church's structure. We also host leadership nights three times a year so we can train and teach everybody who serves in the church. The ministry leaders have an onboarding process to initially equip those who sign up, and they have ongoing training (weekly, monthly, or quarterly, depending on the need) for all those involved to keep participants sharp and inform them of any changes in the schedule or strategy. For instance, the greeters may meet for ten or fifteen minutes before people start to arrive to pray together and discuss anything they need to know for that day. The leaders in many ministries meet once a month so the leader can give instructions, provide details about upcoming events, and remind them they are channels of God's love and power. A few ministries are seasonal or occasional, so the leaders get their people together before the events, even if it's only a couple of times a year.

I believe most churches wait too long to involve people in groups and serving. The longer people wait to get involved, the more they'll think it's abnormal. We have a wide-open door to bring people in, and we created a very short path to get connected to classes, groups, and service opportunities. From the day they trust Christ, we explain they're now part of Christ's body, and for the body to be healthy, all of us need to participate to strengthen every part. We don't wait until they're trained before they start serving. Instead, we release people for ministry right after Next, and they then receive on-the-job training. Our philosophy is "go-ready-set" instead of "ready-set-go."

The first person John records that Jesus sent out was a Samaritan woman despised by the Jews and an outcast to her own people. And the first one in Matthew's and Mark's accounts had only moments before been naked, living among the dead, and demon-possessed. Jesus healed the man and told him, "Go home to your family and tell them how much the Lord has done for you, and how he has had mercy on you." Mark tells us, "So the man went away and began to tell in the Decapolis [ten cities] how much Jesus had done for him. And all the people were amazed" (Mark 5:19-20). The first missionary needed an offering for clothes before he could go! If Jesus thought a woman who was outcast and a very recently demon-possessed guy were ready, we can trust Him to use people who haven't yet completed comprehensive training.

Pastors can have either fast-growth problems or slow-growth problems. In many ways, it's our choice.

Pastors can have either fast-growth problems or slow-growth problems. In many ways, it's our choice. Slow-growth problems are a lack of motivation, bickering over petty things, and far more knowledge than enthusiastic obedience to God's call to be light and salt. Some people have attended church for decades, but they have no impact (at least not a positive one) on their friends and neighbors. They don't dream about making a difference for Christ and expanding His kingdom. Instead, they dream about winning the fight about the color of the carpet.

Fast-growth problems are very messy, like the Corinthians Paul chided for letting a guy sleep with his stepmother (1 Corinthians 5:1-5). Now that's a messy fast-growth problem, but I'm glad Paul gave us help on how to handle it! Yet I'll take fast-growth problems any day because people are excited about what God is doing in them and through them. If we need to talk about whether to put ashtrays outside the entry so newcomers will feel at home, I'm completely good with that! If people are asking, "How do you pray?" or "How can I figure out how to read the Bible?" or "Do you let anyone come to your church?" or "What if I don't believe like you do?" and similar questions, we're on the right track. But if unbelievers and new believers who are rough around the edges don't feel comfortable with us and never come back, we've missed the heart of God for them.

Certainly, not all roles are open to people who are just beginning their relationship with Christ or aren't mature in their faith. At River Valley, we believe teachers and leaders need to be mature and grounded, but those who serve in most capacities need only to be willing, available, and obedient. The end of the pipeline where we release people is *immediate* (they don't need training to sign up and start), *continual* (they always look for new opportunities because every role is temporary), and *progressive* (as they grow in their faith and gain experience in serving, many will want to take leadership roles).

Everyone can serve in a *general* way, like cleanup days, and "Serve Your City" events. Then we should all try and find our place in a *gathered* way when we assemble on the weekends or weekdays for worship services. Lastly, I think we should serve in a *specialized* way using our individual skill sets. What a great way to add value to all that God is doing to build His church. (Recently I asked web designers, programmers, and "quant jocks" to help us build the church by investing their unique skills to improve our digital platforms!)

Of course, when Christians move to our community and begin attending our church, we want to connect with them and get them involved in the pipeline as soon as possible. We realize some have been wounded by the leaders of another church and others have served so long and hard that they're burned out. They sometimes tell me, "Pastor, we just want to chill for a while. We need a break, so we're not going to get involved right now."

Invariably, I reply, "You're not here to chill out. You're here to get involved."

After the shock wears off a bit, I explain, "Some time ago I had a heart attack. Right after the doctors stabilized me, they wanted me to get going. The very next day they told me to get out of bed and start walking on a treadmill because moving was the path to physical health. I was thinking to myself, *I just had a heart attack! Shouldn't I be lying around?* Not according to my doctors! Unless patients are deathly ill, doctors want them up and moving. If they remain immobile, their health problems will multiply. That's my advice to you. Even if you're burned out, don't check out. Even if you're wounded, get moving, get serving, because it helps you get healthy! You don't need to carry the weight of the world on your shoulders, but get involved, meet people, and let God use you. Doing nothing usually leads to more and bigger problems, so find the appropriate level of involvement for you. That's the path to spiritual health."

Beyond Our Walls

Many pastors, especially those overseas, have no intention of releasing people to plant other churches or be involved in ministries outside the church. Their strategy is "catch-train-keep," not "catch and release." They are blind to the benefits—to the broader kingdom of God as well as their own churches—of creating an environment that inspires people to dream big dreams, listen to God's voice, serve with passion, and go wherever God leads them. I believe God will reward me more for the people we've sent beyond River Valley than for what happens at our church. I want to be faithful and openhanded as I respond to God's call to dream, pray, and send people far beyond our walls. When God uses us to train and send someone to serve in India or to plant a church across town, their impact is part of our church's legacy. God isn't going to look only at what we're doing at River Valley and say, "Well done, good and faithful servant." He'll say that, undoubtedly with more joy, as He sees how the people we send have an impact for the gospel in the lives of people our church would never touch.

Abraham's inheritance is all the faithful people and communities that have sprung up since he believed God, and mine is all the faithful people and communities our church has had a hand in launching. When people tell me they sense God calling them to a ministry away from our church where there's great need, I'm not threatened or jealous—I'm thrilled! Their obedience is the greatest mark of blessing on me and our church. And wherever those people go, they take our DNA of an expansive vision and the joy of releasing people to believe God for more.

We're trusting God to send out 500 missionaries from our church to every corner of the world. We call it "The Missionary

Action Plan" (MAP). We're teaching the participants how to get out of debt, how to identify their passion and gifts, and which mission agencies align best with them. As of 2018, we've sent about 100, and we have over 180 in the MAP pipeline. We pray for, equip, and support those people. We ask them for a minimum of one year on the field, and we ask them to pray about making a lifetime commitment. When we launched this effort, some of our highest capacity leaders told us they had heard God's voice and they wanted to go. Each of them was going to leave a hole at River Valley. I remember praying, "Lord, do You really have to call the best?"

I sensed God tell me, "Give Me your best, and I'll take care of everything."

In that moment, I prayed, "Lord, You can call anyone you want. They're all Yours."

Sending people and creating holes in our church is the new measure of success. I'm not just willing to send them; I'm overjoyed our church is exactly what God has called us to be. I think every denomination should give awards for the churches that *send* the most people, not to those that *keep* the most people. In this way, we will bring the good news of Jesus to the whole world!

I think every denomination should give awards for the churches that *send* the most people, not to those that *keep* the most people. In this way, we will bring the good news of Jesus to the whole world!

As we send some of our best people and they leave gaps that need to be filled, two things have happened: other people have stepped up to fill those gaps, and I've had to wrestle with my pride. At pastors' conferences when I learned about the size of other churches, I've prayed, "Lord, we could grow so much more if we kept those great people!"

And in a flash, the Lord said, "Are you kidding Me? Those people are going where there is no church, there is no gospel, and the people don't have anyone to tell them about Me. You may not be building *your* church as big as you'd like, but you're building *My* church exactly as I'd like. I love that you're sending those people out into the harvest field where there are so few laborers. That's your calling. Don't forget it."

In building His church, we have a wide funnel at the opening of our leadership pipeline to go to them and invite them to come to Christ. As we "catch" them in God's net of grace, we notice how He has wired them, we point them to His purposes, and we release them to do whatever He has called them to do. Every time we see someone take a step away from selfishness and toward God's calling and His cause, my heart soars.

Think about it:

1. What are several ways churches can have a wide-open funnel at the beginning of the pipeline? Which ones do you think can be productive for your church? Explain your answer.

2. How well do you relate to unbelievers in your messages every
    Sunday? What are some specific things you can do to relate
    more effectively so your people will be excited about inviting
    their friends and neighbors to church?

3. When people come to Christ, how does your church give
    them assurance, the basics of how to pray and read the Bible,
    and an invitation to serve? How well is it working? How can
    you tell?

4. Do you think asking people to serve very early in their church
    experience is risky? Why or why not?

5. In your church, how and when are people trained for specific roles as they serve?

6. What are some examples of the problems related to slow growth? What problems are related to fast growth? Which of those characterize your church? Which do you *want* to characterize your church? What, if anything, needs to change?

7. What are some reasons (almost certainly hidden) that many pastors don't want to send people beyond their own walls?

8. What are the benefits to you, your church, and the Kingdom to have a vision beyond your own church?

PART 3

ONLY *GOD*

CHAPTER 7

CHANGE OF HEART

In 2002, our church was about seven years old. We had started as a portable church, and then we rented space in the warehouse. At this point in our church's life, we could sense that it was time to buy our own building. I was very excited about the future! I met with a banker in my office to begin talking about the kind of loan we'd need. He looked carefully at our financials, and then he told me, "I have some bad news. You don't have enough money coming in, you have no money in your building fund, and you have too much debt."

Well, I already knew all that—especially the part about the debt. I had financed the church on my and Becca's credit cards. (It was the only way we could get the church up and running at the time, but don't tell Financial Peace founder Dave Ramsey!) Every time we bought something, it was in my name on my credit. I was on the hook for about $100,000 . . . at 21 percent interest! (I don't advise this for anyone else, yet it's part of my story I wouldn't change.)

The banker could tell I was devastated, but he didn't offer any pastoral comfort. He concluded, "I hate to break the news to you, but you're not going to be able to buy a building."

His words were a body blow. If we couldn't buy a building, we couldn't grow; if we couldn't grow, we'd stagnate; and if we stagnated, we'd either die or become irrelevant. A fearful future flashed before my eyes. I had tried to do what God had called me to do, but it looked like it was all going down the drain. We'd hit a wall. I had no answers. It looked hopeless.

In about five seconds I went from being a man filled with faith to being totally crushed, but there was no point belaboring the situation. I stood up, thanked the banker for meeting with me, and escorted him to the lobby. As we walked out, I noticed a couple who had been coming to our church for a couple of months. They were in the reception area waiting to talk to me, but they didn't have an appointment. As soon as the banker left the building, I realized I needed to put on a good front for the couple, so I instantly switched from darkest depression to God's man of faith and power! I walked over to them and said, "Hey, good to see you. I was just talking to the banker about getting a loan for our new building." I was smiling on the outside, but I was dying on the inside. I asked, "How can I help you?"

The wife said, "Actually, we want to talk to you about giving a big gift to the church."

I said, "That's great. Just write the check and put it in the offering this week."

She looked a bit puzzled and after a few seconds said, "Okay, but it's kind of a big gift."

I went to DEFCON 2: "Then you can give the check to our business manager so the ushers and anyone else in the congregation won't see it."

She repeated, "Okay, . . . but it's a pretty big gift."

That was the third time she had used the term "big gift," so I was very curious. I asked, "Well . . . how big is it?"

She said, "We need to tithe half a million dollars."

My mind jumped to DEFCON 5. I thought, *Does she mean the tithe is* on *half a million dollars or the tithe is half a million dollars? There's a big difference!* Both are wonderful, but one changes the month and the other changes the trajectory of the church.

They explained together, "We've had a business deal for $5 million pending for a couple of years, and it's going through now. We want to give $500,000 to the church."

My mouth said, "Thank you," but my heart said, *You just saved the day! This is a miracle!*

The woman told me, "Oh, don't thank us. Tithing is obedience."

We talked for a few more minutes, and they left. I was in awe.

Don't miss this! The *problem* had been in my office while God's *miracle* was waiting in the reception area. The problem and the solution walked past each other. I think God gathered the angels and told them, "Hey, come watch this. You'll love it! Rob has no idea what I've been orchestrating behind the scenes. This answer is going to blow his mind and show him I'm more involved in his life and ministry than he can imagine!"

There are some problems that I need to fix, there are some problems others need to fix, but there are some problems that only God can fix. This was one of them. In this moment, I learned that God loves His church far more than I do. If *I* do my part, and *they* do their part, *God* will do His part. Breakthroughs require the presence and power of God.

When we think about trusting God for great things, we can make one of two errors: trusting Him too little or trusting Him too much. We trust Him too little when we don't believe He can or will step in. God often asks us to trust Him when everything visible screams that the situation is hopeless, and we believe our eyes more than we believe God. But we can also trust God too much, assuming that for God to get the credit He has to act completely apart from human agency. We expect God to drop a sack of money on our doorstep instead of moving people to give generously. It often takes time, experience, and maturity to figure all this out, but God is the Creator and King of the universe, so nothing is impossible for Him. His ways are inscrutable, and He often acts in ways that don't make sense to us, but He's not a genie in a bottle who will pop out and do tricks for us. Many people ask God to intervene with a miracle, and they're disappointed when He doesn't come through. We need to make certain, though, that we're doing our part and they're doing their part first . . . before we expect God to do what only He can do. The groundwork by us and them leads to the dramatic, unmistakable breakthrough.

When we think about trusting God for great things, we can make one of two errors: trusting Him too little or trusting Him too much.

Deep faith trusts God for miracles but doesn't demand them. If we learn to depend on Him, sometimes (but not always) He'll orchestrate circumstances so minutely that a business deal that has been pending for years comes through and a dear couple comes to see us at the exact moment when a banker has delivered devastatingly bad news. That's not a coincidence; that's God!

From our perspective, God often seems painfully slow and timid, but God's power and purpose are always far above what we can imagine, and He operates on His timetable, not ours.

If we take too much responsibility for what happens, we feel pride when things go well and shame when they don't. But when things have gone well, we humbly realize God has been gracious enough to use us, and we give Him the credit because He is the source of wisdom, power, and grace to enable us to do what He has called us to do.

In the 19th century, Robert Murray McCheyne traveled and preached in Scotland. After he saw people come to Christ in response to his sermons, he got on his horse and rode out of town. When he was out of sight, he got off his horse, knelt beside the road, and ceremoniously took an imaginary crown off his own head and put it on Christ's. This was his way of reminding himself who gets the credit.[13] Our failure to give God the credit due Him isn't just a minor mistake. Ask King Nebuchadnezzar how it worked out for him! We don't want to be out in the field eating grass because we patted ourselves on the back too much. (See Daniel 4.)

But we can have a very different problem: trusting ourselves exclusively. One Christian leader commented that he can be busy in his office all day and never think about God. This man, and to some extent many like him, go through the motions of pastoring and leading without any sense of God's magnificent power. When pastors can identify all three columns of responsibility, they know what God has given them to do, and they delegate more easily. And when they believe God can do miracles, they experience periodic breakthroughs that inspire, amaze, and transform everyone who knows about them. We're not doing ministry in our own strength; we're partners with the almighty Creator and King!

Sometimes, only God can touch people's hearts so they give generously or come through in some other way, but at other times, God changes what seemed to be hardened hearts.

City Council

When we received the gift of $500,000, we paid off our credit cards, gave $60,000 to world missions, put $250,000 in our building fund, and used the rest for our operating budget. Within a couple of months, I began looking around town for a site where our church could buy or build. The best option we could find was an old, shabby dollar theater that had the noxious odor of stale popcorn and urine. But then one day the owner of the warehouse where we'd been meeting asked if we might be interested in buying his property. We were leasing about 26,000 square feet in a building of about 60,000 square feet. If we bought it, we'd have room to grow. I had no idea he would even entertain the thought of selling the warehouse. He told me, "I own many buildings in the Twin Cities, and this is the only one I'm willing to sell. If you want it, I'd like to sell it to River Valley." He didn't give me time to catch my breath before he asked, "Do you have the money to put down on it?"

I asked, "How much do you need?"

"$250,000. That's about five percent of the selling price of $4.8 million. I'll finance the rest myself."

I was so excited! To complete the transaction, I needed permission from the city Planning and Zoning Committee. I made the proposal and felt confident we were moving forward, but their response was an unequivocal "No!" The head of the committee explained that they were happy for us to rent the space, but if we bought it, the building would no longer generate tax revenues for the city. I've heard this is a very common reason why cities turn down churches' applications. It is, I'm convinced, very short-sighted because churches do far more good for the community than the cities lose in tax dollars. On balance, the cities come out ahead.

I was committed to make this deal work, so I planned my strategy. I knew that we'd be rejected by the Apple Valley city council because they would accept the recommendation of the Planning and Zoning Committee. After that, I planned to reapply. For the second meeting, I was going to ask every person who is supportive of River Valley Church to pack the meeting room and let our city council know they were in favor of our church buying the warehouse. I envisioned a traffic jam on the streets outside, a crowd inside the room, and an overflowing mass of faith-filled humanity in the outer hallways. If they turned us down again, I was going to lawyer up and fight the city in the courts.

But first, I was prepared for step one: the initial meeting with the city council. They had the Planning and Zoning Committee's recommendation in hand, and I was ready for them to turn us down. In fact, members of the city council had already told me privately that our petition was a lost cause, and they had no intention of approving the sale. They explained that the city already had too many properties that weren't contributing to the tax base: The Minnesota Zoo, a park of hiking trails, a regional park, new school buildings, a number of churches, and other nonprofit properties. Their explanations didn't give me even a sliver of hope, yet I wasn't going to go quietly. I was going to tell them we would reapply and hire attorneys to fight for us. As I walked in that night, I was locked and loaded!

Minutes before the meeting began, representatives from our church took our seats. The agenda showed that our request was far down the list of items the council would cover, but when the chairman gaveled the meeting to order, he announced that he was changing the schedule. He said, "I want to start with the request from River Valley Church."

I thought, *Okay, he can't wait to give us the thumbs down, so he's starting with us!* I was already angry and ready to jump in to object to their decision.

The chairman smiled at us and announced, "We want you from River Valley to know that we love your church. You've done so much good in our community." (We had hosted two funerals for city officials because they anticipated large crowds and the other churches weren't big enough.) He continued, "You obviously love our city." He picked up the Planning and Zoning report and then said, "We've changed our minds about your request. We met just before this meeting and decided to approve the sale of the property to River Valley."

I almost stood and yelled, "I object!" because I was so keyed up. Then I realized this was the answer to our prayers! The chairman was happy to give us the miraculous news, but then he shook his head, smiled, and added, "Please don't try to buy any more property in the city. This is the limit."

The change of heart God orchestrated in the private meeting of the city council before the public meeting didn't come out of nowhere. God used our church's outreach in the community, our care for people outside our church, and the reputation of our faithful people as data points in the minds of the city council members. The miracle came in the context of pastors and church members taking responsibility and faithfully fulfilling God's call. The groundwork led to a breakthrough. I did my part, they did their part, and God did His part!

Whose Victory?

God will always do His part, but some Christians expect God to do *their* part. Their personal philosophy is "Pray and wait," but in the vast majority of cases, God's command is "Pray and work." In only a few places in the Scriptures, God tells people to stop working and start watching. One of those times was on the banks of the Red Sea. God had sent ten plagues to force the pharaoh to release them from slavery, and they plundered the riches of Egypt as they left. But Pharaoh had a change of heart and sent his army to capture them. At the sight of the most powerful army in the world, the former slaves were terrified. They complained to Moses, "Was it because there were no graves in Egypt that you brought us to the desert to die? What have you done to us by bringing us out of Egypt? Didn't we say to you in Egypt, 'Leave us alone; let us serve the Egyptians'? It would have been better for us to serve the Egyptians than to die in the desert!"

In *The Ten Commandments* we see one of the most dramatic moments in cinematic history depicting one of the most dramatic moments in all of history. God told Moses to raise his staff and hold out his hand, and God parted the sea for the people to cross on the dry seabed. Moses told the quivering crowd, "Do not be afraid. Stand firm and you will see the deliverance the Lord will bring you today. The Egyptians you see today you will never see again. The Lord will fight for you; you need only to be still" (Exodus 14:11-14). For good measure, God set a time limit on the miracle. As soon as the Israelites got to the other side, the miracle ended as the Egyptians were driving their chariots across the seabed. The waters rushed back, drowning the entire Egyptian army.

Far more often, God uses human agency to accomplish His will. I think of the equation that an infinite God needs some kind of integer to multiply himself through. Even if we're only a one, the limitless power of God can work in and through us, but infinity multiplied by zero is zero. God is just looking for one person to multiply His infinite resources through! All of God's resources are available if His people, even those who aren't as sharp as others, trust Him to do what only He can do.

God is just looking for one person to multiply His infinite resources through!

A short time after the Israelites crossed through the Red Sea, they were attacked by the Amalekites. Moses sent Joshua, his general, to enlist an army to fight them. The writer of Exodus tells us:

> So Joshua fought the Amalekites as Moses had ordered, and Moses, Aaron and Hur went to the top of the hill. As long as Moses held up his hands, the Israelites were winning, but whenever he lowered his hands, the Amalekites were winning. When Moses' hands grew tired, they took a stone and put it under him and he sat on it. Aaron and Hur held his hands up—one on one side, one on the other—so that his hands remained steady till sunset (Exodus 17:10-12).

Who won the victory that day? "So Joshua overcame the Amalekite army with the sword." But his victory was undoubtedly God's victory. The Lord told Moses, "Write this on a scroll as something to be remembered and make sure that Joshua hears it, because I will completely blot out the name of Amalek from under heaven" (Exodus 17:13-14). Moses was responsible for his part in listening to God and relaying directions, Aaron and Hur did their part in supporting Moses (literally), Joshua was responsible to do his part in leading the army, the men in the army were responsible to do their part of fighting, and God did what only God can do.

Miracle-Shaped Prayers

Understanding the three columns of responsibility profoundly shapes our prayers. We trust God for a vision that requires much more than human effort can produce, but we recognize that God uses us to accomplish His goals. We ask God to lead us, empower us, and use us. We're the willing and faithful integer for the infinite God to work through. This humbles us, inspires us, deepens our dependence, and gives everything we do eternal value because we're God's valued partners!

Paul grasped the wonder that infinity is looking for flawed people who are willing partners. Early in his first letter to Timothy, he wrote:

Here is a trustworthy saying that deserves full acceptance: Christ Jesus came into the world to save sinners—of whom I am the worst. But for that very reason I was shown mercy so that in me, the worst of sinners, Christ Jesus might display his immense patience as an example for those who would believe in him and receive eternal life. Now to the King eternal, immortal, invisible, the only God, be honor and glory for ever and ever. Amen (1 Timothy 1:15-17).

The breakthroughs God gives me may not happen often, but they powerfully remind me that I can trust God for amazing things. I'm never alone, and I'm never out of resources. My worst day can become my best day. God can turn even bad situations— like the Israelites trapped on the banks of the Red Sea or the city council members first assuring me there was no hope our deal would be approved—into something that builds my faith, stimulates others to trust God for more, and shines a bright light on the glory of God. When I remember those moments, I have more faith to trust God during the next dark day.

I fully expect to see God produce breakthrough moments. If I'm doing my part and our people are doing their part, I'm convinced God has all He needs to work in a way that is beyond anything we could imagine . . . and I'm convinced He delights to show himself in these ways!

I fully expect to see God produce breakthrough moments. If I'm doing my part and our people are doing their part, I'm convinced God has all He needs to work in a way that is beyond anything we could imagine.

When I read about people of faith in the Scriptures and in church history, I realize they had very different personalities and lived in widely varied circumstances, but they all had one thing in common: they were willing to live on the edge and take risks. It's very easy for pastors and other church leaders to organize their lives and ministries so they don't have to trust God. They stay busy doing good things and helping people, but far too few let themselves get into a position that if God doesn't come through, they're toast. When we signed the deal to buy the warehouse, the man who sold the property and financed it demonstrated great faith. I hope and pray our church will always listen to God's voice and trust Him for things that amaze people when He answers. When I realized this man was trusting God so much, I told our staff and our leaders, "We need to stretch our faith muscles, live bigger, and trust God for much more than before! We can't have the landlord living by more faith than we are!" I expect God to give us breakthroughs, and I want to lead in a way that raises the expectations of everyone around me.

Develop a Track Record

Over the years, God has a remarkable track record of miracles—not little ones, but dramatic ones—in my life and in our church. I could write a history like Psalm 105 of the list of miracles God performed when He released His people from slavery in Egypt. It wasn't just one miracle, but a long series of them! That's what my life has become.

When I speak at conferences and share some of these unparalleled answers to prayer, pastors sometimes tell me, "You must be one of God's favorites." What they mean is that God certainly won't do things like that in their lives! Sometimes I point them to Romans 2:11 and assure them God has no favorites, or more accurately, we're all God's favorites. (As you read this, if you're thinking "Not me," stop right now. You can be sure that your loving heavenly Father is very fond of you!) As I talk with them and try to find out what they're thinking and believing, I often uncover past disappointments when God didn't come through like they hoped He would, and their painful experience gives them an excuse to avoid the risk of trusting Him today. They looked like a fool once, but never again. When doubt replaces faith, they operate in their own strength, redefining ministry as administration instead of vibrant spiritual leadership. I tell them, "Stop making excuses and believe again in the God of breakthroughs. Raise your expectations. Take the risk of believing God for great things. Put yourself in a place where the only thing that can accomplish the purpose is a genuine miracle, and believe God for one."

I also caution others about comparing their situations with mine or with others. Our church needed God to move in a couple's hearts to give us $500,000 so we could buy a building, but the pastors who talk to me at conferences may need only $5,000 or $50,000. For them, that's every bit as much of a breakthrough as God giving us half a million! Actually, God's miraculous provision for our church was progressive: the first gift was $5000, the next was $55,000, and then we received the $500,000. I certainly didn't complain that the first two gifts weren't as big as the last one. Each of them was undeniably from the hand of a gracious and generous God. Today I'm asking God for a $5 million gift. (Let's just keep adding a zero to the progression!)

Comparison kills. I want to encourage leaders to believe God for more, but we veer off track every time we think, *I want God to do for our church what He did for that one.* We need to listen to God's voice, do what God has told us to do, trust Him for a breakthrough, and let Him determine the outcome. We need to stop preprogramming God's miracles. We can envision them to some degree, but we need to leave room for an infinitely wise, powerful, and creative God to work His will in His way—which may be very different from what we want Him to do. Look to Him, not other pastors (and certainly not me) for the measure and timing of the breakthrough. Be willing to take risks (and sometimes look like a fool) so that you put yourself in a place to see what seemed impossible become a reality.

We need to stop preprogramming God's miracles.

The Right Column

As I've written in earlier chapters, I had a very difficult time figuring out who is responsible for what. Most of the time, I put far too much in my column, and the weight of it all threatened to pulverize me. Because I was doing so much, I didn't give others the benefit of sharing the load so they could grow in faith and skills. I was in their column too. And frankly, when I was running like crazy, I thought very little about God's column. I'm sure I got in His way when I tried to do His job for Him. I didn't have three columns; there was only one, and "Rob" was written at the top.

It was during this period that we had the debacle of our contractor stealing money for the buildout at the warehouse. Becca called everyone in the church to encourage me, and that evening saved my sanity. As the fog cleared, God showed me that I had to have more than one column to survive. If everything stayed in my column of responsibility, I wouldn't be any good to anybody.

I told Becca and those dear people that night, "I'll never do this again. Being a general contractor definitely isn't in my gift mix. It's not how God can use me to advance His kingdom. Somebody else has to step into this role." I finally realized—the hard way, of course—that I needed people to serve in their column, and I needed to trust that God was present and powerful in His column.

The transition was necessary, but it wasn't easy. I told our board that I wasn't going to be in charge of the next building program. That decision scared me to death, but I knew it was right. And it happened: God brought godly and competent people to serve in their column. Through their outstanding service, the church grew. And occasionally, the only hope for a person or a situation is for God to come through—sometimes, to change fixed minds and melt hardened hearts.

I suspect I may not be the only pastor who has struggled to have more than one column.

Think about it:

1. How would you describe the effects of each of the two errors: trusting God too little, and trusting Him too much?

2. How can you determine when it's good and right to "pray and wait" and when you should "pray and work"?

3. What are some signs pastors have redefined their jobs to be busy in administration as an excuse to avoid believing God for miracles?

4. What are some underlying reasons why leaders stop believing in God's ability or willingness to provide breakthroughs? Which of those have affected you? Explain your answer.

5. What does it (or would it) mean for you to live on the edge and take risks to trust God for far more?

6. Are you willing to look like a fool on occasion? Explain your answer.

7. In your life and ministry, how much is in God's column? Is it the right amount? Why or why not?

CHAPTER 8

ORGAN DONOR

When I held my prayer retreat and God led me to make our church multi-site, you may recall that I needed a bit of reassurance. That's when God told me that someone would give us a church building as a sign. Two days after I announced this direction to our staff team, someone called to offer a building in Fairbault, Minnesota . . . which was one of the towns where God had led me to put a Post-It note as a future site of one of our campuses.

It all looked as smooth as silk, but only for a short time. I assumed I would just show up and the church leaders would say, "Thank you for coming, Pastor Rob. Here is the signed deed, and here are the keys to the church. It's all yours." It wasn't quite like that. The person I had talked to on the phone was very positive, but he explained that the church board and some members wanted to interview me before they made a final decision. He explained that most of the people in the church knew they needed to become a campus of a larger church to survive, but a few still needed to be convinced.

Fairbault is only about thirty-five miles from Minneapolis, but I'd never been there before. When several of my staff and I drove into the town at about 4:00 in the afternoon, we found the church pretty easily. It was a very typical small-town church, with a steeple and a cross on top. From my first glance, I could tell they had deferred maintenance for a long, long time. The roof was missing some shingles, there were gaps in the siding, and the shrubs were overgrown. The four remaining deacons took us on a tour. The youngest of them I'm guessing was about 65. The interior looked more like a funeral home than a church, with mauve paint on the walls and swirling colors in the floral pattern carpet. The congregation had dwindled over the years, and by this time, less than half the building was being used in any capacity. In fact, they had recently moved their worship services to the smaller fellowship hall, and the sanctuary was empty every Sunday. In the basement, I was surprised to find what looked like a Goodwill warehouse. The deacons told me that members of the church used it to store their unused furniture.

I asked the deacons what had prompted them to call us and offer to become one of our campuses. One of the men started to tear up as he told me, "Pastor Rob, there aren't any people in our church who look like you and your staff team." (He was talking about how young we were.) One of our staff members had brought her baby. The deacon pointed to the child and said, "I want to hear babies cry again in our church." He paused for a second and then added, "I want to wash children's fingerprints off the windows again." At that moment, all their deacons were crying, and so were we. We all agreed it was a beautiful "God moment."

Our meeting the next evening was a chance for every member (about forty people) to come to meet us, hear from us, and ask questions. I discovered they were considering two other churches as partners, so it wasn't a slam dunk by any means. As I stepped into the lobby before the meeting, I heard God say to me in my spirit, "Tell them it says 'organ donor' on your driver's license."

I thought, *Oh man, that's really weird!* And I prayed, "Uh, Lord, is there anything else You want to tell me about this? I don't think You've given me all the info!"

But God was silent. I tried to imagine why I'd had such a strong impression, but I couldn't shake it. It was obvious this very strange line was something God wanted me to tell them . . . but when? . . . and why? And did I mention, it was weird!

I gave my presentation to the group and invited questions. It was obvious that a faction sitting near the back was hostile to me and our church. They had their arms crossed, and the look on their faces screamed, "Over my dead body!" There was, I was sure, sadness mixed with the anger. They had devoted their lives to this church, and it had come to this moment when they needed help to keep the doors open. On our tour the previous afternoon, the deacons had been positive, and the people who sat near them seemed equally optimistic that this arrangement could work well for everybody. The current pastor and his wife were there, but they weren't really engaged. They were planning to leave the church as soon as the deal—any deal—was done.

Some of the questions about the multi-site model were straightforward, the kind you'd expect anyone to ask. Then one of the men in the back stood up and growled, "Our building is worth a million dollars. I want to know what your motive is for being here."

At that moment, I sensed the Holy Spirit say, "Tell them now."

I took a deep breath and announced to him and everyone else in the room, "On my driver's license, it says that if I die, I'm an organ donor." I had no idea what to say after that sentence, but the Holy Spirit downloaded what came next: "When I die, I want the doctors to take everything useful in me and give it to the living who need it. I don't want anything of value to be buried in the ground. If my heart can save someone, take it. If my liver can save someone, use it. Kidneys, lungs, eyes, and anything else— use them to save someone, but don't bury them." I paused for a second, and continued, "This church has an opportunity to be an organ donor. You can give what's valuable and useful in this church to River Valley, and we can use it to grow and thrive. Your heart is in this church. Give it to us, and the church will live and reach this city. It will be your heart, but it will be beating in the chest of River Valley Church. Don't bury all God has done in your church. Sure, you can refinance the building and use the money until it's all gone and then someday sell it as an art center, but you and others didn't give sacrificially to this church for it to become an art center. You want to reach people for Jesus, and you can do that if you donate what's valuable to us."

The man who had been so angry and defiant looked around the room and almost laughed. He said, "I say we vote right now!" And they did. Of the forty people, 36 voted for the proposal to become one of our campuses, two voted against it, and two abstained.

That night the Post-It note on the map became a River Valley campus. Today, about 450 people worship at that church every Sunday. Hundreds have come to Christ through the witness of the people in that church, and some of our strongest staff have come out of its ministry. The church is full of joy, life, and the power of God to change lives. You'll hear the sounds of babies, and deacons have to wipe fingerprints off the walls . . . and no one seems to mind.

After the meeting that night, some of my staff told me, "That thing about being an organ donor, that was genius!"

"No way!" I explained, "That was entirely from God. I didn't plan to say that at all. I just heard the voice of the Spirit tell me to say it, and I said it. That's all. I could never have come up with something that timely and that profound on my own! God's insight led to the breakthrough."

Daily Manna

The children of Israel didn't face Pharaoh's army with their backs against the Red Sea every day. That was an unusual threat and a dramatic, one-time rescue. Thankfully, we don't face impending disasters every day either! In the wilderness, they needed God's provision every day. He miraculously provided manna, water, and quail. Those acts of God gave them life, sustained them when they had nothing else to eat, and reminded them that God was actively involved in their lives.

As leaders (and spouses and parents and friends) we need God to continually give us insights to redirect us and steer us in the right direction. It was no less a miracle when God told me to tell the people in Fairbault that "organ donor" is written on my driver's license than when the couple came by with the gift of $500,000 at exactly the moment when the banker who had rejected us was walking out, or when God changed the hearts of the city council so we could buy the warehouse.

Sometimes people say they're impressed with some of the decisions we've made at our church, but in almost every case, the ideas came as impressions from the Holy Spirit. Yes, I'd been thinking, and yes, I'd been praying, but I don't think I could have come up with those innovative ideas on my own. My theory is that if I'm moving and committed to obey, I'm more open to God bumping me to a different path or a little farther along on the same path.

A lot of pastors see themselves primarily as organizational managers who orchestrate programs, people, and meetings. They pray, but they don't expect God to break in and answer! Instead, we need to see ourselves as beloved children who expect our Father to communicate with us. Then, we'll expect Him to show us when we're drifting, and we'll expect Him to delight in us when we trust Him. That's how fathers treat the kids they love! Pastors can build a pretty good church if they are primarily managers. They use the same principles as any person in business who launches and builds any enterprise. The pastors may have a very clear sense of what they're responsible for and what their people are responsible for, but they often give only lip service to God's presence and power.

A lot of pastors see themselves primarily as organizational managers who orchestrate programs, people, and meetings. They pray, but they don't expect God to break in and answer!

I'm not trying to be critical. It can happen to any of us. We work hard, and we pray—but something happens, either suddenly or gradually, that makes us think God isn't really all that involved in what we're doing. We become tired and disappointed. We don't sense the Spirit, yet we keep trudging on. After a while, we're living in a new normal. We don't tell anybody we've given up on the supernatural intervention of God in our lives and ministries. We still talk a good game, but our hearts don't believe it any longer. In the past, we were spiritual leaders who trusted God for more than we can ask or think, but that's a distant memory.

The Plan and the Presence

When I ask pastors if they're listening to God as they lead, some try to change the subject, some nod but don't really want to talk about it, and others say, "We're working our plan."

I tell the last group, "That's great, but there's more. As you implement your plan, you can listen to the voice of God and get directions from Him."

They often give a half smile and respond, "That would be great. I wish I could count on Him to do that." Many of them follow up by asking, "Tell me how that works for you. How can I learn to listen to the Spirit like you do?"

I don't believe we need to be some kind of Super Pastor to hear from God. We only need receptive and responsive hearts. In a good marriage, the husband and wife get to know each other so well they get on the same wavelength and anticipate each other's thoughts and desires. In the same way, as we grasp more of God's truth and grace and get to know His heart, we'll anticipate His whispers. Soon, listening to God becomes second nature. We expect to hear from Him! We still plan, we still organize and delegate, but we also listen for divine interruptions.

How does God communicate with us? He's far more creative than we are when we try to connect with a spouse and friends. In a *Crosswalk* article about ways to hear from God, Whitney Hopler observes:

You may sometimes hear God's message in dramatic ways, such as through angels, visions, or miraculous
events. But more often, you'll hear God speaking through
your thoughts. . . . God will use dramatic means to get
your attention when necessary, but His goal is for you to
be so closely connected to Him that you'll pay attention
whenever He speaks to you. Usually, God speaks through
what people have described as a "still, small voice" to encourage those He loves to choose to keep walking closely
with Him through life.[14]

Prayer is more than a list of desires we rattle off to God each
day. In a rich and real relationship, we listen as much as we speak,
and we're not concerned about checking all the boxes. Intimacy
and connection are more important than being sure we've covered
every base. Pastors who see themselves as managers are content
with prayer lists because they can be completed, but pastors who
see themselves as children of the King delight in being with Him,
expect Him to break in with insights, and aren't shocked when
He points them in a direction they'd never imagined before. If I
went to my father and said, "Hey Dad, here's a list of the things I
want you to do for me," first, he'd be offended that I see him as a
vending machine instead of a person, and then he'd take the list
from my hand, put it down, and say, "Son, tell me what's on your
heart, and let me tell you what's on my heart."

God seldom breaks in with undeniable statements like the
one about being an organ donor. More often, He dialogues with
me in passages of Scripture, through sermons by gifted pastors
that expand my concept of God and His purposes, in times with
my mentor, through Becca's insights, and in object lessons from

the circumstances I face. In all of those, I can be dense and unresponsive, or I can be open, receptive, and eager to obey whatever God tells me to do.

These aren't rare occurrences. Virtually all of my best sermons are the result of genuine dialogue with God about a topic, a passage, or a spiritual principle. As I immerse myself in the Scriptures and meditate, I'm not in a hurry to finish. It's much more important that I take time to listen, consider, and explore what God puts on my heart. Very often, a thought comes (seemingly) from out of the blue that pulls the whole message together. That's not blind luck, it's not magic, and it's not the effect of coffee—it's the power and presence of the Spirit as I expect Him to communicate with me.

Virtually all of my best sermons are the result of genuine dialogue with God about a topic, a passage, or a spiritual principle.

My journal is a chronicle of intimacy with my Heavenly Father. We share with each other, and I'm learning to be a better listener. I'm a beloved child of the King, not because I've earned it but only by the gift of His grace. There's no arrogance in that; it's confidence. It's humbling to realize everything good in my life comes straight from the hand and heart of a loving, attentive God who's involved in every aspect of my life. As I read, pray, and write in my journal, I'm usually not trying to write sermons, but ideas and concepts surface in those times that form the heart of my messages.

Such times of reflection before the throne of God have become normal conversations with Him, and they have trained my heart to be receptive to the unusual times when God breaks in to give me specific directions. The instruction about telling the church in Fairbault that I'm an organ donor wouldn't have registered as more than an off-the-wall thought if God hadn't already cultivated a receptive heart in me over many years. As I lean into Him in my devotional times, I sense His heart, so I'm not surprised when He gives me directions to step into a situation with a word from Him.

Becca has been right with me every step of this journey. When we started River Valley in 1995, we had nothing: no building, no equipment, and very few people. We needed about $75,000 for a sound system, video equipment, and some other essentials. We also needed to buy enough equipment to at least have a portable church, but there was a big problem: we had no money.

I had been the youth pastor at a church in Milwaukee when I sensed God call me to plant a church. They agreed to send me $200 a month, and I had about $800 a month in other pledges. I went to our bank and asked for a loan of $15,000. They turned me down. I went to another bank, and another, and another. The loan officers at seven banks all said "No."

I was sure God had called me to plant a church, but I needed a breakthrough. I realized I had five Visa Gold cards in my wallet, and each one had a $20,000 limit. Why five banks had given a youth pastor gold cards is a mystery to me, but they did. (When I went to a restaurant with my youth pastor friends, I sometimes threw the five cards on the table when the check came. They were so impressed, yet I still hoped one of them would pay—or at least split—the bill.) I told Becca that I was going to buy everything we needed: "Honey, the Lord provided. I'm putting it all on my Visa Gold cards!"

She wasn't thrilled, so she said, "Okay, but I want to see how the Lord is involved in this instead of it being just your big idea to start a church."

"What are you talking about?" I thought I knew, but I wasn't sure.

She explained, "God has to bring in at least $20,000 to show that He's in this. When that amount comes in, you can put the charges on the credit cards."

Instantly, I had a goal to pray for. I was sure God could give us that amount of money, no problem. I would tell people about our church plant, and someone would write us a check. I decided the best place to go was God's family, the churches in the area. Surely, they'd be thrilled to help. They weren't. Almost all of them said they were at the limit of their resources. They had little to no money to invest in a church plant.

Weeks passed, and very little came in. We had set our launch date and scheduled ads in the newspaper to invite people to come to our opening. I had to order the equipment by a certain date so it would arrive in time, and that deadline rapidly approached. Finally, it was D-Day. Portable Church Industries in Michigan closed at 5:00 in the afternoon. As I prayed that morning, I sensed the Holy Spirit say, "You have the money. Go ahead and order the equipment."

I thought, *This is awesome! It's going to happen!* A couple of hours later, I went to the mailbox to open the letter with the check for $20,000. Nothing. I waited all afternoon for the FedEx or UPS truck to pull in front of my office. I wanted to walk down the street to meet them on the way, but I resisted that urge. Neither one came. At 4:55 p.m., it was go or no go. If I didn't order the equipment in the next five minutes, we'd have to delay the launch and we'd have egg on our faces. Check that, on *my* face.

All afternoon, I had sensed God say again and again, "You have the money. Order the equipment." Now He was yelling it to me! I picked up the phone and called Portable Church Industries to place my order. I told the salesman, "God has provided the money. Please start my order." He started praising God, but I quickly hung up. I didn't want him to ask how we got the money.

I went home and told Becca, "I called and ordered the equipment."

She was so excited: "Did you get a miracle? We got the money?!"

I tried to evaporate quickly into thin air. All I could say was, "Sort of."

"What do you mean 'sort of'?"

I told her, "Today in prayer, I felt the Holy Spirit tell me, 'You've got the money. Order the equipment.' I obeyed. Great, huh?"

It wasn't hard to tell that she wasn't buying it. "So, you *didn't* get the money," she deadpanned.

"Technically."

She wasn't reassured, so I said, "He told me we did, so we're good."

Becca fired back, "You broke the agreement. We said . . ."

I interrupted, "No, I didn't. I heard the voice of God so clearly: we have the money."

We sat down for dinner, and Becca was stabbing her food like she was stabbing me instead of the chicken on her plate. I was grateful the chicken took the brunt of her frustration.

In the middle of the tense, silent meal, the phone rang, and I jumped up to answer it. It was a staff member at another church in the city. He said, "Last night our church voted to give you a $35,000 no-interest loan. I've had the check sitting on my desk all day. I'm leaving on vacation tomorrow so I've had a long list of things to do today, and giving you the check is the only thing I didn't get to. Do you want to swing by and pick it up tomorrow morning?"

I almost shouted, "Yes! Yes, I do!"

When I hung up, I turned to Becca and celebrated, "We've . . . got . . . the . . . money!"

After we danced in the kitchen, the Lord spoke to me again: "I knew they voted last night. I want you to listen to Me when I speak to you that clearly. I need you to be obedient. Function in every gift I've given you, and be attentive to My voice so you can build the kind of church I want you to build."

I replied, "Got it. I'll listen better."

This moment reminded me (and God continues to remind me) that I'm not building *my* church, and I'm not building a nonprofit organization: I'm building God's church, in His way, according to His leading, and with His love and power to change lives. Christ is the cornerstone, not some set of organizational principles. Christ in us is the hope of glory, not our slick marketing.

Finding Treasure

When pastors hear me speak on the importance of listening to God's voice, some come up and say, "Pastor Rob, I used to hear from God, but it's been a long, long time. What can I do to get back there?"

I tell them to go back to those things they were doing when they heard God more clearly, and this time, "Tell Him you'll treasure whatever He tells you to do." They're often surprised with that term, so I explain, "Tell Him you'll value Him and His leading more than anything else, you'll steward whatever He says to you, and you'll obediently act on His directions."

This commitment is both thrilling and threatening. As God's children, we long for an intimate relationship with Him, but we're well aware that He may (almost certainly) tell us to do something that scares us to death. In those moments, we need our concept of God to be expanded.

In C.S. Lewis's *Chronicles of Narnia*, Aslan the lion is a Christ figure. In a remarkable scene, Lucy asks Mr. Beaver about Aslan:

"Is—is he a man?"

"Aslan a man!" said Mr. Beaver sternly. "Certainly not. I tell you he is the King of the wood and the son of the great Emperor-beyond-the-Sea. Don't you know who is the King of Beasts? Aslan is a lion—*the* Lion, the great Lion."

"Ooh!" said Susan, "I'd thought he was a man. Is he—quite safe? I shall feel rather nervous about meeting a lion."

"That you will, dearie, and no mistake," said Mrs. Beaver; "if there's anyone who can appear before Aslan without their knees knocking, they're either braver than most or else just silly."

"Then he isn't safe?" said Lucy.

"Safe?" said Mr. Beaver; "don't you hear what Mrs. Beaver tells you? Who said anything about safe? 'Course he isn't safe. But he's good. He's the King, I tell you."[15]

The writer to the Hebrews invites us, "Let us then approach God's throne of grace with confidence, so that we may receive mercy and find grace to help us in our time of need" (Hebrews 4:16). We can go to Him confidently, but we should never forget that we're coming to the throne room of the King who reigns over the entire universe. He is the Creator of "things in heaven and on earth, visible and invisible, whether thrones or powers or rulers or authorities; all things have been created through him and for him" (Colossians 1:16).

When God breaks in to give us instructions, they're not suggestions.

When God breaks in to give us instructions, they're not suggestions. He loves us dearly, and Jesus died to ransom us out of the domain of darkness and deliver us into the kingdom of God, but we're not spectators. We're God's children who have been called to follow Him wherever He may lead us. This is the challenge Jesus gave His disciples and us: "Whoever wants to be my disciple must deny themselves and take up their cross and follow me. For whoever wants to save their life will lose it, but whoever loses their life for me will find it. What good will it be for someone to gain the whole world, yet forfeit their soul? Or what can anyone give in exchange for their soul?" (Matthew 16:24-26)

It wasn't just a good idea (or a crazy idea) for me to tell the people in Fairbault that I'm an organ donor. It was God's directive. In effect, God was saying, "Be ready. Here's what I want you to say. Even though it doesn't make sense now, it will then. And watch how I'll use it."

Another piece of advice I give pastors who want to learn to hear God better is to analyze the voices they're listening to every day. I need to do the same thing. I can get so wrapped up in listening to negative people that my optimism can fade, and I can listen to political talk radio so much that my outrage darkens my outlook. When I realize that this is happening, I step back, turn the volume of those voices down (or off), and turn the volume up on messages that stimulate faith, hope, and love. I listen to great pastors teach the Word of God, I tune in to worship music, or I talk to a friend who restores my sense of balance and sanity. The question for all of us is: how long does it take to realize the voices we hear aren't spiritually enlightening? If it takes too long, negative and angry voices become normal, and we stop unplugging them and looking for better ones. Even great leadership books can cause us to depend on organizational principles alone instead of depending on God as we use those principles.

When we're confused or not sure if we've heard God clearly, we should look for a confirming second voice. My mentor, Sam Chand, is that voice in my life. All of us need a mentor, coach, pastor, or wise friend who will listen patiently and ask great questions to help us clarify what God is saying to us. We don't need someone who jumps in to give us "the answer." That's not helpful. We need someone who knows how to bring out the best in us and help us discern the voice of God among all the competing voices.

Occasionally, I need help to discern what God is saying to me, but God sometimes speaks so clearly that it's unmistakable. When I get messages like the one in the Fairbault church lobby and on the day when I needed to order equipment, I tell Becca and I may tell a few others, but I'm not looking for confirmation—I just need them to hold me accountable.

Young leaders sometimes come to me with an idea that they aren't sure is from God. After I hear them, I often say, "That lines up with your gifts, it meets a specific need, and God has given you some great insight about how to meet it. I think you've heard from God!" But occasionally, someone tells me how God might be leading, and I say, "You might want to go back and listen again. I don't see how it lines up with how God has created you." Those may be hard words to hear, but God has made me a sounding board for them, and it's my responsibility to listen prayerfully and offer my perceptions.

When I read the Bible, I see God speaking to people from beginning to end. Certainly, there were times when God seemed absent, like the 400 or so years of slavery in Egypt and between Malachi and the birth of Jesus, yet in most cases God communicated with His people very clearly. I don't think things have changed today. I love Luke's account of Paul's being redirected by the Spirit:

Paul and his companions traveled throughout the region of Phrygia and Galatia, having been kept by the Holy Spirit from preaching the word in the province of Asia. When they came to the border of Mysia, they tried to enter Bithynia, but the Spirit of Jesus would not allow them to. So they passed by Mysia and went down to Troas. During the night Paul had a vision of a man of Macedonia standing and begging him, "Come over to Macedonia and help us." After Paul had seen the vision, we got ready

at once to leave for Macedonia, concluding that God had
called us to preach the gospel to them (Acts 16:6-10).

The Holy Spirit stopped them from preaching at one place,
prevented them from going to another place, and then gave Paul a
vision to travel to another continent, Europe, to tell people about
Jesus. How did he respond? "We got ready at once to leave for
Macedonia, concluding that God had called us to preach the gospel to them." They didn't sit around wondering what they should
do. Paul had a track record of God's clear leading, and he was instantly obedient . . . and he trained the people with him to listen
and be obedient! That's the mark of a spiritual leader.

You may already have that kind of relationship with God, or
you may have lost it and are longing for it again. No matter where
you are in your journey, God wants you to know Him intimately—so intimately that you sense His presence, respond to His
nudges, hear His voice when He speaks, and obey Him even when
it doesn't make sense. Spiritual growth makes us more aware of
our wrong motives so we can confess them, and it makes us more
in tune with God's heart so we want what He wants. God is infinite, so the future is always present to Him. He has orchestrated
rescue and blessings for His beloved children. It's our privilege to
be older brothers to the people in our churches to help them hear
God and obey Him, like Paul modeled for Luke and the others
around him. We can be very good organizational leaders, but God
wants more for us. He wants us to be spiritual leaders in every
sense of the term: cleansed by God, led by God, empowered by
God, and used by God to change lives.

We can't manufacture this kind of spiritual life on our own.
God has to produce a tender heart and a listening ear in us.

If we follow Him in this way, we'll see Him work in ways that are unmistakable. Ironically, we'll get more applause for those breakthroughs than anything else we do, but we know where the praise belongs, so we gladly shift it to Him.

When God redirected Paul to Europe, it wasn't in a vacuum. God had already given Paul directions for his missionary journey to take the gospel to the provinces of Asia. He was working the plan when God broke in to change his plans. As we're faithful and obedient to God's call, He sometimes redirects us. That doesn't mean we were disobedient or off base. It means we serve a wise and loving but inscrutable God whose plans are always bigger than we can imagine.

As we're faithful and obedient to God's call, He sometimes redirects us. That doesn't mean we were disobedient or off base. It means we serve a wise and loving but inscrutable God whose plans are always bigger than we can imagine.

Define what you're responsible to do, delegate to others who will share the load, and expect God to do what only He can do, including a change in direction from time to time. God will do His part, but usually only after we've proven faithful to do our part and we've equipped others to do their part. That's the family environment in which the Father delights to lead His obedient children.

Think about it:

1. Are you satisfied with the frequency and level of God speaking to you? Why or why not?

2. What are some differences between leading an organization and being God's beloved child helping to run the family business? How do those differences shape our expectations of how the Father instructs us?

3. What are some specific examples of how God has spoken to you during the last month through:

    • the Scriptures?

    • a mentor or friend?

    • your spouse?

    • an object lesson from an experience?

4. What are some of the voices in your world that threaten to drown out God's voice? Why do you keep listening to them? What benefits do you get? What are some negative effects?

5. What are some voices that reinforce your faith and optimism? When do you listen to them? When do you need to listen to them?

6. How do you know when you need a second confirming voice, and when God's instructions are unmistakable?

7. In what ways is listening and obeying God thrilling? In what ways is it threatening?

8. What is your prayer now, at the end of this chapter?

CHAPTER 9

BIG BOOM

At times our efforts come up empty, the people around us are impotent, and our only hope is to echo Isaiah's prayer: "Oh, that you would rend the heavens and come down, that the mountains would tremble before you!" (Isaiah 64:1)

Sooner or later, all followers of Christ have a Red Sea moment, and not necessarily because we've messed up and caused the calamity. The children of Israel hadn't disobeyed God. They had seen God perform miracles to bring plagues so the pharaoh would set them free, and they responded in faith when Moses led them out of Egypt. Still, as they stood on the banks watching the mightiest army on earth roar toward them in chariots, they lost all hope. They were terrified, they felt betrayed, and they were ready to go back into slavery! They had been slaves only days before, and now they faced certain death . . . unless God did something supernatural, miraculous, stupendous, and shocking . . . which is exactly what He did.

The parting of the sea was a big boom! After the Israelites crossed to the other side and watched the waters come rumbling back and drown their Egyptian pursuers, they were incredibly relieved. Moses and Miriam sang a wonderful song of praise to God for His deliverance. Several psalms remind God's people how He rescued them when they had no hope. I can imagine Jewish families telling this story throughout their history, and it's part of our history too because we're grafted into the story of God working in, for, and through His people.

All of us face heartbreaking moments which seem like a towering, insurmountable wall, and we can't find a way over it, under it, around it, or through it. We may face the effects of a tragic accident, a dreaded diagnosis, a crippling addiction, a financial crisis, a prodigal child, or a marriage that's in tatters. In most cases, we never see it coming, but when it happens, it consumes every waking moment—which is just about all day and all night.

Overcoming Bitterness

Strained and broken relationships are incredibly painful. During a season at our church, I had ongoing conflict with one of our staff members who was leaving to take another position as an evangelist. We had been very close. I had officiated at his wedding, we had helped him and his wife through some very rough marital waters, and I let them live in my grandfather's condo when they needed a place to stay. But a tension developed between us over a misunderstanding about funding from our church, and it escalated far beyond reason. He became my enemy and an enemy of our church—and hundreds of people knew it.

For years, I tried to resolve the problem, but we were like two boxers who went to our corners every night but came out swinging the next morning. It only got worse when a church became open and needed a pastor, and our church tried to acquire the church as a campus. At the same time, unbeknownst to us, he was candidating to be its new pastor. They decided multi-site was not their plan, so we moved on as a church, but it only escalated the tensions.

At one point, he contacted our denomination's local superintendent and insisted that I was unethical and should be disciplined, maybe even legally. Why? One day the water line from the furnace humidifier in our home broke, and our basement started to flood. Becca called to ask me to do something . . . and fast! I was out of town so I called our business administrator to ask our custodian to please go to my house and stop the leak. (I didn't know it was the humidifier at the time.) He drove to my house and turned off the water. Simple fix, problem solved.

However, the guy who despised me heard about it and accused me of violating the IRS code against using church employees for personal gain. He also accused me of speaking poorly to the board of the church where he was candidating. I assured him that wasn't true, but he insisted I had maligned him in my communication about his church. I told him the opposite was the case: the board of the church asked me about hiring him, and I gave a positive recommendation. (Even with the tension between us, I truly thought he would be a good choice for them.) He barked back, still insisting I had spoken and written against him. No matter how I tried to smooth things over, our relationship was always full of disagreements and sharp barbs.

Every day, I wondered what new drama would arise, until I realized the conflict was consuming me and harming the church—not just the church I lead, but *the* Church. So he and I wrote a co-authored letter to everyone in our two churches and to people across the nation who knew about the strain in our relationship. The letter explained that we had come to a Paul and

Barnabas situation where our disagreement was so fierce that we could no longer work together. We had tried to find common ground, but we had hit an impasse, and we had to go our separate ways. When we finally ended the relationship, I had a gnawing, painful suspicion he would hate me for the rest of his life. I certainly didn't want him or anyone else to feel that way about me, but no matter how hard I'd tried to bridge the gap and trust God to reconcile us, nothing had made the slightest dent.

Years later, long after I had given up hope of any restoration, God intervened and told him that he needed to get right with me and the church. He approached me at a ministers' gathering, and I thought as he walked up to me that he might punch me in the face. But he stopped and said, "Pastor Rob, God spoke to me. We have to resolve the problem between us. God told me we have to make this right." He apologized for his part of the conflict. I forgave him, and the incredible blessing of reconciliation began. I apologized for the things I had done and love pushed out the bitterness we both had felt for so long. Trust overcame doubts and honesty replaced manipulative game-playing. We sent out another letter to tell people what God had done in our relationship. Now, he and his wife spend time with Becca and me, and we genuinely love and respect each other. Only God could have turned such emotional darkness into the brilliant light of renewed friendship. Only God . . .

Another appropriate analogy from Acts is the broken and restored relationship between Paul and John Mark. The young man had traveled for a short time with Paul and Barnabas, but he bailed on them. When Barnabas wanted to give John Mark another chance, Paul refused, which led to their parting ways. We don't hear much about John Mark for a long time, but perhaps fifteen years later, Paul wrote and told Timothy: "Get Mark and bring him with you, because he is helpful to me in my ministry" (2 Timothy 4:11). At some point, John Mark and Paul were reconciled, trust was restored, and John Mark became a valued colleague again. That's what happened between me and my old nemesis, who again became a dear friend.

A survey conducted by The Fuller Institute, George Barna, Lifeway, Schaeffer Institute of Leadership Development, and Pastoral Care Inc. reports that forty percent of pastors experienced "serious conflicts with a parishioner at least once in the last year," and seventy percent "do not have someone they consider to be a close friend."[16] In another survey, over eighty percent of pastors reported they had failed to resolve conflict with a staff member, board member, or key volunteer.[17] And at home, things are no better: seventy-seven percent of pastors report discontent in their marriage.[18] No wonder so many of us often feel like we're in the soup all alone.

Plenty of pastors have tried diligently to step into these messes and find God's grace and strength to resolve them, but they've failed. The only hope is for God to give them a miracle.

Plenty of pastors have tried diligently to step into these messes and find God's grace and strength to resolve them, but they've failed. The only hope is for God to give them a miracle. That's what it took for my friend and me to be restored. If you find yourself in that place now, as much as it depends on you, be at peace with all people and make the move to reconcile the relationship. If it's not your move, pray for a miracle and never lose faith. God can bring peace into any storm.

Just One Cow

Money problems may also need God's intervention. I've told several stories about how God has provided for us financially. Let me share another that is one of my favorites.

At one point, our church finances were incredibly tight. I kept a close eye on every dime we spent, and I prayed like crazy that God would move our people to give generously. But the day came when we were close to the bottom. I prayed, with a touch of frustration, "Lord, You own the cattle on a thousand hills. Why don't You sell just one of them and give the money to us!"

A few days later, I received a card in the mail. When I opened it, I found a check for $1000. The note read: "Pastor Rob, I was driving by a field of cows today, and the Lord told me to send you a check for a thousand dollars. He told me to be sure to tell you where I was when He prompted me to send this check to you."

I love that. God had a sense of humor when He stepped in to provide money for us. He could have done it a zillion different ways, but He chose to provide in a way that was unmistakably His hand at work. There was no way in the world that this could have been a coincidence. It was only God.

Welcome to Holland

When our eldest son Connor was born, Becca and I couldn't have been more thrilled. We enjoyed every moment of his early months. When he was about two, my mom would watch him three days a week so I could work selling appliances while I started the church and while Becca was working full-time to support our family and my calling. After a day or so, Mom found the boldness to tell us, "I'm afraid Connor isn't developing like he should. You may want to have someone look at him."

I insisted, "Oh, Mom. He's just shy. There's nothing wrong with him." But then she gave me "that look," and I knew she was serious.

Connor slept only if we kept him in a car seat. Every day, we brought the seat into the house so he felt comfortable enough to go to sleep. If he wasn't in it, he cried for a long time before he fell asleep. We couldn't take the disruption night after night, so we set up the seat in his crib and let him sleep in it, tightly buckled in. Becca and I thought it was kind of cute, but Mom saw it as a symptom of a bigger problem.

She pointed out some other concerns: At every meal, Connor sat in his high chair and turned everything into a train. He lined up every particle of food on his plate. If he opened a toy in the kitchen and played with it there, it was the only room where he would play with it. If I brought it into the living room, he took it back to the kitchen. When we took his picture and said, "Cheese," he ran to the refrigerator looking for a piece of cheese. He almost never made eye contact, and he only parroted back whatever we said to him. He didn't have any personalized concepts or statements. He didn't interact with other kids at church or at the park. For the first year he was in the nursery, we were paged almost every week because he bit other children. We were planting a church, but we were losing young families because their kids were afraid of Connor. That wasn't so cute.

When we took him to a specialist, we heard the word we never expected to hear: autistic. We were devastated, but we were determined to give Connor every advantage possible. We put him in special education classes and for two years Becca and I prayed, fasted, and read every book we could find on healing. We took him to church services, festivals, prayer meetings, and every other event where someone might touch Connor so the power of God would heal him. Nothing. Not a hint of change. Time after time, we walked in full of hope, but we walked out demoralized.

After many such disappointments, my expectations and prayers changed. I began to believe that Connor would never be healed, and that God is a loving Heavenly Father who would give us strength to bear this burden. I didn't blame God as harsh or unkind, but I concluded that for some reason He was unwilling to heal our son. I wasn't angry with Him, but I no longer believed He would give us a miracle.

During this dark time, Becca and I read a short story called "Welcome to Holland" by Emily Perl Kingsley. She begins, "When you're going to have a baby, it's like planning a fabulous vacation trip—to Italy. You buy a bunch of guide books and make your wonderful plans. The Coliseum. The Michelangelo David. The gondolas in Venice. You may learn some handy phrases in Italian. It's all very exciting." She continues to explain that the child's birth is like the plane ride to the wonders of Italy, but when the plane lands, "The stewardess comes in and says, 'Welcome to Holland.'"

"Holland?!?" you say. "What do you mean Holland?? I signed up for Italy! I'm supposed to be in Italy. All my life I've dreamed of going to Italy."

Gradually, it dawns on you that there are no options of now traveling to Italy, yet Holland isn't so bad. They even have Rembrandts.

But there's a problem . . . a big problem. Everyone else is going to Italy, and they're quick to tell you how wonderful it is there. You're glad for them, but it feels empty, wrong, hard. You can't help but think, *That's where I'm supposed to be!*

Kingsley concludes that the pain of being in Holland will never go away because it's the loss of a cherished dream. However, if we spend our lives shrouded in grief and might-have-beens, we'll miss the joys offered to us in Holland.[19]

Becca and I cried and cried when we read this story. It perfectly described our initial joy, our high hopes, our deep despair, and our resolve to make the best of things with Connor. We were in Holland, not Italy, but we were going to enjoy it as much as we could. We prayed, "Lord, this isn't where we wanted to be, but we trust that You'll give us wisdom and courage to face every setback. Welcome to Holland." Healing was off the table. Hope for a miracle was history. We were moving on with our lives. God had said "no," and we needed to accept His answer.

A few months later, we had a visiting pastor, Bill Peppard, come to share his testimony of God saving his life. It was a bizarre set of circumstances: The night after his daughter's wedding, Bill had been shot by a masked intruder with a shotgun. (Incidentally, Bill's son-in-law was the staff member with whom I'd had such painful conflicts, but before our falling out I had officiated at his wedding.) The slug went through Bill, through the wall, and into the backyard. When EMS rushed him to the hospital, an Indian doctor looked at Bill and said, "He must be a holy man." It was obvious to this ER doc that my friend's father should have been dead, but God spared him. The police never caught the gunman.

It was a wonderful service. After Bill shared his story, a lot of people came down to the front for Bill to pray for them. Meanwhile, I began loading up the portable equipment and packing it in the truck. Finally, Bill had prayed for the last person, and he came over to Becca and me. She was watching Connor. I thanked him for sharing his story, and he asked, "Is there anything I can pray for the two of you?"

The words "more church growth and more tithing" were forming in my mouth, but Becca jumped in: "Our son has autism, and we want God to heal him."

At that moment, my wife was like the woman who asked Jesus to heal her daughter, and when He hesitated, she told Him, "Even the dogs get the crumbs that fall from the table." Becca was that woman who wouldn't take "no" for an answer! You have to understand that this was way out of character for Becca. She is so gentle and kind, but at that moment, she was a fierce mama bear. I chimed in, "Yeah, that's what we want you to pray for," but I was thinking, *Uh, I thought we'd given up on that. Remember, "Welcome to Holland"?*

Bill smiled and put his hands on Connor. After a few seconds, he said quietly, "I feel this is from the Lord: God is going to heal your son for His glory." He paused and then told us, "God has seen that you believe He's a loving God, but He's going to show you that He's a powerful God. He's going to heal your son."

At that moment, our four-year-old son, who had never made significant eye contact with us, looked up at Becca and me and said, "Hi, Mom. Hi, Dad." Like the story of Pinocchio, the boy came alive! Then he said, "Where are we going now?" He wasn't withdrawn, and he wasn't just parroting us. God had done it!

The rest of the day, Becca and I couldn't stop crying and talking. Connor was acting like every other kid his age! We were stunned. Words can't describe our joy and gratitude. We called every member of our family and all our friends who had prayed with us and for us. It was a glorious day! This wasn't just a marginal healing; Connor was completely restored.

The next morning, we took Connor to his special education class. We called teacher Pam over and said, "Check him out."

In an instant, she could tell he had radically changed. She almost yelled, "What happened to Connor?"

Becca told her, "He was healed in church yesterday." She was thrilled!

Pam left the room to tell her boss what God had done. Her boss wanted to test Connor for autism. It took a little while, but when she was finished, she walked into the room where Becca and I were waiting. I was shocked at her words. She snarled, "This child is completely normal. He doesn't have autism. How dare you waste taxpayer money on special education for your son for the last two years!"

I replied, "Yeah, it's every parent's dream to rip the state off through special ed!" I calmed down after a couple of seconds, and then I told her, "Our son was healed by God in church yesterday."

She sneered, "I don't believe in that."

We walked out of the school with more joy than ever. A year later when we took Connor to be screened for kindergarten, we didn't say anything about his past condition. After the testing was over, the teacher said, "Your son is ready for kindergarten."

I asked, "Did you notice anything that might cause you to be concerned? Any red or yellow flags?"

She looked curious and shook her head, "No. No, nothing at all."

"How about, oh, maybe autism?"

"Not at all. Why?"

I wanted to say, "Oh, no reason," but I told her, "Because he had autism and was healed by God a year ago."

She shook her head, "No, there's no sign of it at all. He didn't have autism."

I wanted to say, "Yes, he did!" but I just smiled as we walked out of the room. That was about twenty years ago. During all those years, there has never been the slightest return of any of the symptoms that dominated our lives for those four hard years. Today, Connor is a normal twenty-something and is the Connections Pastor at River Valley Church. He coordinates the intake and assimilation for every person who comes to us. When I look at him, sometimes it's hard to remember what life was like before God gave us the big boom. But I want to remember because it reminds me that God isn't only a loving God, He's also an immensely powerful God!

Already and Not Yet

During the period when I gave up on God's willingness to heal, I reduced God to just a little smaller than the size of my problem. I believed He *could* fix it, but that He wouldn't. After Connor was healed, I realized my faulty view of reality doesn't limit God's love and power. The reality of God's greatness and grace never diminishes, even though my hard reality seems bigger than Him.

When I was trying to be content "in Holland," people asked me to pray for them or a loved one who was very sick, often dying of cancer or some other terminal disease. I put my hand on them and said, "Lord, if You want to heal this person, please do that." Yet as I was praying, I was thinking, *But I don't think You will. You're a loving God, but You really don't heal any longer. You'll heal him in heaven, but not here. Welcome to Holland.* And I finished, "In Jesus' name, amen." I had become a chaplain to comfort people, but I had abdicated my role as a pastor empowered by God to trust Him for miracles.

I reduced God to just a little smaller than the size of my problem. I believed He *could* fix it, but that He wouldn't.

One day God spoke to me: "Don't let your circumstances limit My power." I realized we live in the overlap of ages: The old age was before Christ came, and it was characterized by sin, sickness, and death. When Jesus came, He announced the inauguration of the kingdom of God! As we look around at all the suffering, sickness, violence, and selfishness, we wonder, "Can this really be Christ's kingdom?" We need to understand that His kingdom has already been inaugurated, but it hasn't yet been consummated. In the coming age when Christ returns, all wrongs will be made right, all sin becomes past tense, all sickness is healed, and all doubts turn to joy as we experience unhindered the love, power, and purpose of God in His glorious presence. In the meantime, we live "between the already and the not yet," a time when some of the promises have been fulfilled, and the rest will be fulfilled "on that day" when we see Jesus face to face.

In Paul's letter to the Romans, he makes two seemingly contradictory statements—contradictory unless we understand this concept of the overlap of the ages. He tells them, "The Spirit you received does not make you slaves, so that you live in fear again; rather, the Spirit you received brought about your adoption to sonship. And by him we cry, 'Abba, Father'" (Romans 8:15). We *have received* the Spirit of sonship; we *already are* children of God.

Yet only a few verses later, Paul writes, ". . . we ourselves, who have the firstfruits of the Spirit, groan inwardly as we eagerly wait for our adoption to sonship, the redemption of our bodies. For in this hope we were saved" (Romans 8:23-24). Here, Paul says that we *wait* for our adoption. Did Paul need someone to proofread this letter? No, he's explaining the truth that Christ's death on the cross has already fulfilled His promise to forgive us, impute His righteousness to us, and adopt us into God's family, but in this life, we look forward to the *ultimate* fulfillment of all the promises in the new heavens and new earth. What does this have to do with praying for healing? Everything!

Jesus' death paid for the healing of every person: "By his wounds we are healed" (Isaiah 53:5). All sickness yields to the power of the cross of Jesus. Wholeness—the complete absence of sickness and suffering—is waiting for us in heaven. This is the truth we cling to: sickness was taken care of on Calvary, and complete healing is promised in the future when we see Jesus face to face. When we ask God for a miracle, we're asking Him to bring some of heaven into our circumstances today. That's what a miracle is: when God brings a taste of eternity into our present.

I used to pray, "Lord, if it's Your will, heal this person." I didn't want to presume whether God would heal now or later, and to be honest, I was pretty sure it was always going to be later. But my prayers have changed: "Lord, I know it's Your will that this person is healed. Now, in Your goodness, would You release the miracle of healing promised in heaven into this person's life now?"

When we ask God for a miracle, we're asking Him to bring some of heaven into our circumstances today. That's what a miracle is: when God brings a taste of eternity into our present.

This certainly doesn't guarantee that every person will be healed on this side of heaven, but it acknowledges that it is God's will—His promise, in fact—to heal. I'm only praying He would move up the schedule. With this perspective, I can pray with absolutely no reservation. I'm completely convinced God is going to heal each person . . . I just don't know when. I tell people, "You're moving closer each day to complete healing. I don't know if it will happen on this side of the curtain or that side, but you can be sure it's coming."

When I talk to pastors about praying in faith for miracles of healing, I tell them that when my kids were little, they often asked me for ice cream. Sometimes they'd say, "Dad, I want some ice cream, but you're probably going to say 'no.'"

That was painful to hear. They weren't presuming that I'm a good and loving Dad. I taught my kids to ask this way: "Dad, you're amazing. In fact, you're the best Dad in the world! I was thinking . . . wouldn't this be a great day for ice cream?"

They got a lot more ice cream with this approach than by assuming I wasn't going to give them any. Of course, they didn't always get ice cream when they asked, but it was never because I was mean or disengaged; it was because we were going to have dinner soon and having ice cream wasn't best for them at that moment. They'd get it later when the time was right.

This is how we should pray for miracles. We begin by saying, "God, You're so good! You give so many good things to Your children. I know it's Your will to heal. That's one of the results of Jesus' death, and it's one of the joys of heaven. Would You move up the timetable? Wouldn't today be a great day for a miracle? Would You bring a taste of heaven into this moment? Wouldn't today be a great day for a breakthrough?" If He gives it, we explode in rejoicing. If He doesn't, we pray, "God, You're a wise and loving Father. If today isn't a good day for a miracle, I'm still going to trust You. And by the way, I'll ask You for it again tomorrow."

I no longer pray, "If this is Your will, please heal this person" because I *know* it's His will. I just don't know His schedule. We may see the miracle today, or we'll see it on that glorious day, but either way, we have rock-solid confidence it will happen. When we believe and pray this way, we aren't consumed with confusion and doubt . . . or gnawing guilt that we don't have enough faith. We recognize that God is both infinitely loving and infinitely powerful, and we trust that He is infinitely wise and knows best when to fulfill His promises. If God chooses not to heal the person now, He has all of eternity to make it up to them . . . after He wipes away every tear and heals every infirmity and disease.

Wouldn't today be a great day for ice cream?!

Think about it:

1. In your role as pastor, what are some examples of desperate "Red Sea moments" in people's lives when nothing and no one but God can save the day regarding:

   • strained and broken relationships?

   • financial calamities?

   • severe health problems?

2. What are some of those moments in your own life?

3. What might be going on in our hearts and minds when we allow negative circumstances to limit God's love and power to be a little smaller than our problems? What are some events that might have happened to take us to that point?

4. How might it help you to pray if you have confidence that
   God has promised to heal, and you're asking Him to bring
   some of eternity into today?

5. Is this different from how you've been praying for those who
   are sick or injured? Explain your answer.

6. What pressing, insurmountable problems have come to mind
   as you've read this chapter? Wouldn't this be a great day for a
   miracle?

DON'T LOSE HEART

Recognizing the three clear columns of responsibility—"you," "them," and "God"—has been tremendously helpful to me. With this understanding, I can identify the tasks that God has assigned me as a leader, but I've also discovered I don't have to carry the burden alone. I can delegate responsibility and authority and multiply the laborers going into the harvest fields. I've realized more than ever that I sometimes face situations that require nothing less than the hand of an infinitely loving and powerful God to create a breakthrough.

I've also recognized there's a fourth category, one that isn't as clear and neat, but instead, full of mystery. No matter how hard I work, no matter how gifted and dedicated are the people around me, and no matter how much we trust God, some answers won't come on this side of eternity. When we hit those roadblocks, we're tempted to give up, get angry, or feel guilt that somehow our faith is inadequate (or all three!), so we need a deeper grasp of the sovereignty and mystery of God. Our task is to be obedient to what God has called us to be and do and trust that His thoughts are not our thoughts, and His ways are not our ways (Isaiah 55:8-9).

There's no way we can understand everything God is doing on this side of the veil—He is the all-knowing, all-loving, all-powerful God . . . we're not. I touched on that truth in the last chapter, and I want to expand on it now.

There's no way we can understand everything God is doing on this side of the veil—He is the all-knowing, all-loving, all-powerful God . . . we're not.

When I share the story of Connor being healed of autism, occasionally someone responds, "Pastor Rob, I'm really angry with you."

It has happened often enough that I know what's coming. I usually say, "Tell me about it." And that's enough to open the floodgates.

The person grimaces, "You got your miracle, but I've prayed and prayed and my child hasn't been healed."

I tell him, "I understand completely. I sometimes feel guilty that God answered our prayers and He doesn't always answer the prayers of people who are at least as faithful, at least as dedicated, and at least as prayerful as Becca and me. I didn't do anything different from what you're doing. God didn't reward us because our faith was greater than yours. In fact, I gave up! There was no faith there from me, only Becca! But for some reason, God intervened and healed our son. I can't explain why He hasn't answered your prayers, but it's almost certainly not because there's something deficient in you. Keep obeying God. If He doesn't heal your child here and now, He'll have all eternity to make it up to you. There, you can ask Him how not healing your child fit into His purposes and plans to glorify himself in every one of us. Keep trusting that He is a loving, kind God. Though unanswered prayers for healing stink now, we can trust that God is working things out in His ways for His purposes."

At that point, I usually hug the person and cry with him. I'm told that when evangelist Oral Roberts conducted his healing crusades, he often said that not everyone would leave healed, but he wanted everyone to leave feeling loved. That's a good word for us too.

Two Unchangeable Truths

Though tempted to despair and doubt, we must cling to two truths: God is loving today, and some day everything will make sense. God's love was displayed in neon colors on the cross where Jesus took the punishment we deserve so we could receive the honor He deserves. There is no greater love than this! And throughout the Scriptures, God promises there will be a day when we will be with Him, all tears will be wiped away, we'll experience the unmitigated joy of being His beloved children, and we'll have plenty of time for Him to help us understand what happened in this lifetime.

In Paul's second letter to the Corinthians, he describes the tension between the now and later, the already and the not yet. In this life, we're fragile, but God is with us:

> But we have this treasure in jars of clay to show that this all-surpassing power is from God and not from us. We are hard pressed on every side, but not crushed; perplexed, but not in despair; persecuted, but not abandoned;

struck down, but not destroyed. We always carry around in our body the death of Jesus, so that the life of Jesus may also be revealed in our body (2 Corinthians 4:7-10).

We can have supreme confidence that even if we're weak, God is stronger than all the forces in the universe; even if we don't understand, God is infinitely wise; and even if we falter physically and emotionally, God has us cradled in His hands. Paul describes what this confidence looks like:

> Therefore we do not lose heart. Though outwardly we are wasting away, yet inwardly we are being renewed day by day. For our light and momentary troubles are achieving for us an eternal glory that far outweighs them all. So we fix our eyes not on what is seen, but on what is unseen, since what is seen is temporary, but what is unseen is eternal (2 Corinthians 4:16-18).

If we believe only what we can see, our faith will crumble, but if we cling to God's promises of future glory and restoration, our hope remains strong even when everything is collapsing around us. The troubles that threaten to crush us, as seen from the other side of eternity, are "light and momentary" and are paving the way for us to experience God's glory, affirmation, and joy. In this hope, we can stand, even when we suffer for reasons we don't understand and even when our prayers aren't answered the way we hoped. Novelist Dennis Covington writes, "Mystery is not the absence of meaning, but the presence of more meaning than we can comprehend."[20]

I often think of the people listed in Hebrews 11. The first part of the chapter describes ways God miraculously delivered and provided for heroes of the faith, but that's not the whole story. After a glowing list of God's miracles, the writer reminds us:

> There were others who were tortured, refusing to be released so that they might gain an even better resurrection. Some faced jeers and flogging, and even chains and imprisonment. They were put to death by stoning; they were sawed in two; they were killed by the sword. They went about in sheepskins and goatskins, destitute, persecuted and mistreated—the world was not worthy of them. They wandered in deserts and mountains, living in caves and in holes in the ground.
>
> These were all commended for their faith, yet none of them received what had been promised, since God had planned something better for us so that only together with us would they be made perfect (Hebrews 11:35-40).

We'd love to be like those who enjoyed the magnificent miracles, but perhaps a greater miracle happens when God gives us strength to trust and obey Him when the miracles don't happen.

They were commended for their faith, but in their lives, God's ultimate promises remained unfulfilled. We'd love to be like those who enjoyed the magnificent miracles, but perhaps a greater miracle happens when God gives us strength to trust and obey Him when the miracles don't happen.

If these two truths aren't riveted in our minds and hearts, we easily drift toward comparison. We wonder why God worked in that person's life but not ours, why that pastor sees more people healed that we do, and why that church is growing faster than ours. Comparison is entirely natural, yet it's a deadly poison. None of us is immune to it.

At the end of John's Gospel, we find a touching scene. Jesus appeared on the shore early in the morning while Peter and some other disciples had fished all night and caught nothing. Jesus told them to cast their nets one more time, and they brought in a huge haul of big fish. When they got to shore, Jesus had breakfast prepared for them. We can imagine how Peter felt during the meal. He had promised to be so loyal that he would die with Jesus, but he denied Him to a servant girl and two others as Jesus was being falsely accused and condemned by a kangaroo court. Now, after breakfast, Jesus took him aside. He asked Peter three times, "Do you love me?" And Peter answered each time, "Yes, Lord, I love you." It was a beautiful and necessary reminder of Peter's greatest sin so Jesus could assure him of His complete forgiveness. And with each of Peter's affirmations of love and loyalty, Jesus reinforced his role as a leader in the church: "Feed my sheep." Jesus then explained that Peter would die in the same way, on a Roman cross. At that moment, John walked by, and Peter blurted out, "Lord, what about him?"

I'm sure Jesus wanted to say, "Are you kidding? I just forgave you and restored you to My mission! And you're comparing My plan for you with John?" But He didn't say that to Peter. He only said, "If I want him to remain alive until I return, what is that to you? You must follow me" (John 21:15-23).

That's God's message to you and me when we look at another pastor and implicitly ask, "Lord, what about him?" Jesus has called each of us to follow Him with our whole hearts, but He doesn't have a cookie cutter plan that's the same for all of us. He looks at each of us and says, "Don't worry about him. I have good plans for you. Follow Me."

Cause and Effect

When we ask God for a breakthrough that doesn't come, we look for someone to blame ... and quite often we look in the mirror. We second-guess our leadership, and we doubt our decisions. When Moses realized he had led God's people to a trap between the Red Sea and the Egyptian army, he probably thought, *I am such a loser as a navigator! Look where I've brought us! Where was Waze when I needed it?* And on that lonely Saturday after Jesus was executed on the cross, His followers almost certainly wondered if they'd wasted the last three years, and worse, if they'd be the next ones arrested, tried, and crucified because they had followed Him! They probably asked each other, "How could we have been so wrong?"

More recently, the mother of a child born with a constellation of birth defects wonders, "Is it my fault? Surely, I didn't do something wrong while I was pregnant." If she had been hooked on heroin, that's a possibility, but in many cases there's no clear link between cause and effect. Hard questions that can't be answered can tear a soul—or a marriage—apart. People blame autism on vaccinations, they blame birth defects on the use of forceps, they blame childhood diseases on themselves for not protecting their children, and on and on. The point is that God has given all of us a powerful sense of justice, and we naturally want to find someone to blame when things go wrong. We have to be careful, though, to avoid jumping to wrong conclusions that seem so right.

God has given all of us a powerful sense of justice, and we naturally want to find someone to blame when things go wrong. We have to be careful, though, to avoid jumping to wrong conclusions that seem so right.

When we assume a problem is our fault, we've put ourselves in God's column and insist that we have it all figured out. That's too much weight to bear!

As Jesus and the disciples traveled from one city to the next, they saw a man who had been blind since birth. The disciples were sure there was a clear cause and effect. They asked, "Rabbi, who sinned, this man or his parents, that he was born blind?" Before Jesus made a little clay from spit and dirt, He gave them a lesson in the mystery of God's purposes:

> "Neither this man nor his parents sinned," said Jesus, "but this happened so that the works of God might be displayed in him. As long as it is day, we must do the works of him who sent me. Night is coming, when no one can work. While I am in the world, I am the light of the world" (John 9:1-5).

One of the ironic twists in the story of Connor's healing is that Bill's daughter has an autistic daughter who has never been healed. I'm sure Bill has prayed for his grandchild every day of her entire life. In God's allotment of miracles, wouldn't it make more sense for Him to heal Bill's grandchild instead of Connor... or at least heal the granddaughter first and Connor later? It was and is a mystery to me. Everybody doesn't get a big boom here on earth, but someday Jesus will wipe away everyone's tears, restore everything, and right every wrong.

Closing Thoughts

Here at the end of the book, we've added "mystery" to the other three columns of responsibility. This one is wholly on God, but it focuses on the future instead of today. I want to pray for you. But first, in a spirit of openness and obedience, reflect on these questions and listen to the Lord's whisper.

As you've read Part 1 of this book, what has God said to you about the responsibilities that are in your column, decisions only you can make, and direction only you can set?

I pray that you would step up and own those tasks.

- *Take a minute to write those down as you sit before the Lord.*

As you read Part 2, how did God speak to you about delegating responsibility and authority to competent and eager people?

I pray that you would select well, delegate clearly, train on the job, and celebrate more over others' success than your own.

- *Write what God has said or is saying to you about them.*

As you read Part 3, how did the Spirit whisper or shout that you need to trust Him for a breakthrough only He can provide? Are you ready to ask Him to bring the reality of eternity into the present?

I pray that God will answer your prayers in ways that amaze you.

- *Write what He is saying to you about miracles.*

As you read the conclusion about the mystery of God's will and His ways, what is God saying to you about trusting Him even when things don't make sense?

I pray that God would give you confidence in Him as you live in the middle of mystery. Trust that He is a loving and kind Heavenly Father. Keep working for the "well done" you'll eventually hear from Him.

- *Write what He's saying to you about the tension between what He has already provided and what is promised in the new heaven and new earth.*

My Prayer for You

Father, thank You for my friend who's seeking Your face. Give us an abundance of Your wisdom and grace to be able to put the right people and situations in each of the columns of responsibility. This will require courage to pick up some things and let go of other things, and it will require renewed confidence to trust You more than ever before. I pray that my friend would see You as a loving and kind God, and also as an immensely powerful God. Nothing is impossible for You.

Father, give my friend the strength to keep knocking over obstacles, to keep fighting for the Kingdom, to keep inviting and pushing people to follow You, to love You wholeheartedly, and to trust You more than ever.

Now to him who is able to do immeasurably more than all we ask or imagine, according to his power that is at work within us, to him be glory in the church and in Christ Jesus throughout all generations, for ever and ever! Amen (Ephesians 3:20-21).

ENDNOTES

1   "The Rise of Creativity as a Key Quality in Modern Leadership," David
     Slocum, *Forbes*, January 27, 2015, https://www.forbes.com/sites/
     berlinschoolofcreativeleadership/2015/01/27/the-rise-of-creativity-is-
     a-key-quality-in-modern-leadership/#2036ef587d1a

2   "How a Good Leader Reacts to a Crisis," John Baldoni, *Harvard
     Business Review*, January 4, 2011, https://hbr.org/2011/01/
     how-a-good-leader-reacts-to-a

3   "It Seemed Like a Good Idea at the Time: 7 of the Worst Business
     Decisions Ever Made," Erika Anderson, *Forbes*, October 4, 2013,
     https://www.forbes.com/sites/erikaandersen/2013/10/04/
     it-seemed-like-a-good-idea-at-the-time-7-of-the-worst-business-
     decisions-ever-made/#7acdee243e80

4   "An Employee Dies, and the Company Collects the
     Insurance," David Gelles, *New York Times*, June 22,
     2014, https://dealbook.nytimes.com/2014/06/22/
     an-employee-dies-and-the-company-collects-the-insurance/

5   "Is it ever okay to help a chick out of the shell?" myPetChicken.com,
     https://www.mypetchicken.com/backyard-chickens/chicken-help/Is-
     it-ever-okay-to-help-a-chick-out-of-the-shell-H245.aspx

6   "The Art of Managing Monkeys," Ken Blanchard, September 20, 2010,
     https://howwelead.org/category/one-minute-manager/

7   "Make the most of everyone's time and skills with these 5 tips for
     effectively delegating tasks and responsibility," Peter Economy, *Inc.*,
     August 20, 2013, https://www.inc.com/peter-economy/5-steps-dele-
     gating-wisely.html

8   "Faster than Jackie Robinson: Branch Rickey's Sermons on the Mound,"
     Sam Roberts, *New York Times*, April 13, 1997, https://www.nytimes.
     com/1997/04/13/weekinreview/faster-than-jackie-robinson-branch-
     rickey-s-sermons-on-the-mound.html

9   "Delegating Tasks in the Small Church: Two Options and Six Lessons,"
     Karl Vaters, *Christianity Today*, August 31, 2015, https://www.
     christianitytoday.com/karl-vaters/2015/august/delegating-tasks-in-
     small-church-two-options-and-six-lesson.html?start=2

10   "The 5 Elements of a Strong Leadership Pipeline," Josh Bersin,
     Harvard Business Review, October 6, 2016, https://hbr.org/2016/10/
     the-5-elements-of-a-strong-leadership-pipeline

11   "How Old Is Your Body Really?" Adam Cole, NPR, June 28, 2016,
     https://www.npr.org/sections/health-shots/2016/06/28/483732115/
     how-old-is-your-body-really

12   "Cell Biology by the Numbers," http://book.bionumbers.org/
     how-quickly-do-different-cells-in-the-body-replace-themselves/

13   Cited by Oswald Sanders in *Spiritual Leadership* (Chicago: Moody
     Publishers, 2007), p. 194.

14   "10 Ways to Hear from God Regularly," Whitney Hopler, Crosswalk.
     com, June 15, 2012, https://www.crosswalk.com/faith/spiritual-life/
     how-to-hear-from-god-regularly.html

15   C.S. Lewis, *The Lion, the Witch, and the Wardrobe* (New York:
     HarperCollins, 1950), p. 75

16   Cited by the Pastoral Care Network, http://www.pastoralcareinc.com/
     statistics/

17   Cited by Into Thy Word, 2007 (research from 1989 to 2006) R. J. Krejcir
     Ph.D. *Francis A. Schaeffer Institute of Church Leadership Development*
     http://www.truespirituality.org/

18   Fadling, A. (2009). *Ministry burnout statistics* [Blog]. Retrieved from
     https://anunhurriedlife.org/2009/06/03/ministry-burnout-stats/

19   "Welcome to Holland," Emily Perl Kingsley, 1987, http://www.our-kids.
     org/Archives/Holland.html

20   Dennis Covington, *Salvation on Sand Mountain* (New York: Penguin,
     1995), p. 204.

ACKNOWLEDGEMENTS

A book like this is the product of the heart and labor of many people. Some of these have poured themselves into my life for years. I want to thank . . .

My wife Becca

Thanks for making me your ministry. Thanks for keeping me healthy and whole so that while I was out fixing other things, I didn't need to be fixed! Love you, Shine!

Connor, Logan and Mikayla

Welcome to the family, Mikayla! You're beautiful inside and out. I love my family! Thank you for letting me use you as sermon illustrations. I owe you $5 each!

Our church

To my entire staff and the congregation, thanks for helping me fix the problems, big and small, and being patient when they didn't get fixed fast enough. Our church isn't perfect, but it's healthy and heading in the right direction! Thanks for all you do to turn the vision into reality and reach more people for Jesus!

Dino

Thanks for being the kind of friend who would cosign a loan for a crazy church planter. From Bible college roommates to life-long friends, I know you have my back and I have yours!

Bill

I know Jesus healed Connor, but your prayer of faith along with Becca's changed the trajectory of our lives. Thanks for being obedient to what God spoke to you!

Joe

Thanks for signing off on using our story—as painful as it was, it's beautiful now! I'm praying God will use our mistakes to bring healing to others.

Susan Blount

Thanks for pushing me. My ADD life needs people like you to get me back on track!

Pat Springle

Thanks for helping me write this book. You get me!

Sam Chand

Thanks for coaching, mentoring and being my friend. Your encouragement to make a message into this book is just what I needed! Thank you.

ABOUT THE AUTHOR

As Lead Pastor of River Valley Church, Rob Ketterling is highly regarded for his vision and relentless passion to expand the kingdom of God.

He and his wife Becca have been married for over thirty years and launched River Valley in 1995, which has since grown to over 10,000 people with eight locations across the Minneapolis, Minnesota area.

Rob has a down-to-earth preaching style, allowing his audience to take practical steps in their journey no matter where they are. He inspires people to live an authentic, faith-filled relationship with Jesus, and he challenges leaders at every level to change the world. He is the author of several books including *Change Before You Have To* and *Front-Row Leadership*. He currently serves on several organizational boards including the Lead Team of the Association of Related Churches (ARC) and the Church Multiplication Network (CMN).

Rob loves traveling and spending time with Becca and his family. Rob and Becca have two sons, Connor and Logan, both on staff at River Valley Church. They're thrilled to welcome Mikayla, Logan's bride, into the family. When Rob is not at work building the kingdom, he is recharging on the golf course.

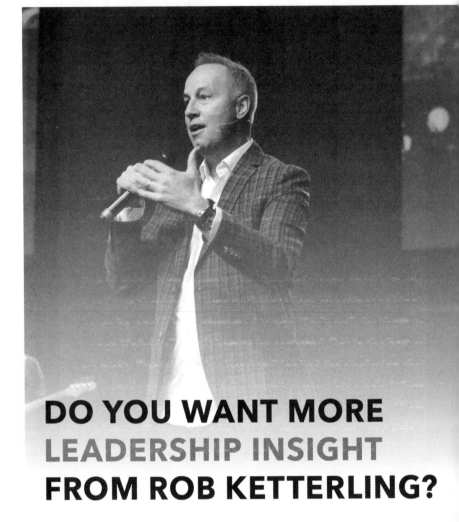

DO YOU WANT MORE
LEADERSHIP INSIGHT
FROM ROB KETTERLING?

We started the River Valley Network for one reason, to help churches succeed and find solutions. We are constantly adding new resources and training opportunities for you and your team. We want to see the local church thrive all over the world and see the Kingdom of God move forward! I hope you will be a part of it.

RIVER VALLEY
NETWORK

Through a relational and practical coaching style, the River Valley Network exists to help bring solutions for your entire team in the areas of giving, church leadership, worship, the next generation and more!

Leadership insights from
Lead Pastor, Rob Ketterling

Access to key staff leading various
ministry areas of River Valley Church

Invitations to regular Leadercasts on
Church Growth, Multi-Site, Kingdom Builders,
and more

Access to Roundtables, one-day Summits,
and special pricing at our annual Conference

Access to a unique collaborative network
of key leaders nationwide

Access to hundreds of unique resources
and creative content including sermon series,
kids curriculum, worship resources, leadership
training, HR documents, and more!

VISIT

RIVERVALLEYNETWORK.ORG

TO LEARN MORE

DON'T DO MINISTRY ALONE.

It's not just about the mission, it's about the relationship we have with God and with each other. Whether you are looking to launch, connect or equip your church, ARC is for you.

WE ARE AN ASSOCIATION OF RELATIONAL CHURCHES WORKING WITH CHURCH PLANTERS AND CHURCH LEADERS TO PROVIDE SUPPORT, GUIDANCE, AND RESOURCES TO LAUNCH AND GROW LIFE-GIVING CHURCHES.

WE LAUNCH

We have a highly successful, proven model for planting churches with a big launch day to gain the initial momentum needed to plant a church. We train church planters, and we provide a tremendous boost in resources needed.

WE CONNECT

We provide dozens of opportunities to connect with other church planters, veteran pastors, leadership mentors, as well as friends who are walking the same path as you are. You're never short on opportunities to connect!

WE EQUIP

Our team continually creates and collects great ministry resources that will help you and your church be the best you can be. As part of this family, you get to draw water from a deep well of experience in ministry.

LAUNCHING, CONNECTING, & EQUIPPING THE LOCAL CHURCH

ARCCHURCHES.COM   @ARCCHURCHES   /WEPLANTLIFE

RESOURCES

To order more copies of *Fix It!* or any of the resources
listed below, go to **resources.rivervalley.org**

Also by Rob Ketterling:

Front Row Leadership

Become the person of influence you were
born to be. Whether you're a CEO, a volunteer, or a homemaker, leadership is
your responsibility. Rob Ketterling offers
tools that will empower you to move up
to the front and lead the change you want
to see take place. Learn to engage the
leadership process and contribute with
your God-given strengths.

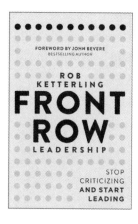

Thrill Sequence

Are you constantly looking for your next adrenaline-packed experience? Seeking another dose of excitement from an adventure with suspense, fun, and danger rolled into one? What if your Christian life were just as thrilling? Rob Ketterling encourages readers to seek adventure in a full-on, reignited faith. He challenges others to discover the excitement in passionately pursuing a life of service and reckless faith.

Change Before You Have To

What will it take for you to change? For most of us, it takes a crisis, a tragedy, a pain so great that change is actually forced upon us. By then, it's way too late. But what if you could find the strength to change before the pain, before the crisis, before the tragedy? No more excuses, no more good intentions, it's time to change and live life to the fullest!